BFI FILM CLASSICS

· ·

Rob White
SERIES EDITOR

Edward Buscombe, Colin MacCabe, David Meeker and Markku Salmi
SERIES CONSULTANTS

Launched in 1992, BFI Film Classics is a series of books that introduces, interprets and honours 360 landmark works of world cinema. The series includes a wide range of approaches and critical styles, reflecting the diverse ways we appreciate, analyse and enjoy great films.

Magnificently concentrated examples of flowing freeform critical poetry.
Uncut

A formidable body of work collectively generating some fascinating insights into the evolution of cinema.
Times Higher Education Supplement

The definitive film companion essays.
Hotdog

The choice of authors is as judicious, eclectic and original as the choice of titles.
Positif

Estimable.
Boston Globe

We congratulate the BFI for responding to the need to restore an informed level of critical writing for the general cinephile.
Canadian Journal of Film Studies

Well written, impeccably researched and beautifully presented … as a publishing venture, it is difficult to fault.
Film Ireland

D1439635

TO BE OR NOT TO BE

Ernst Lubitsch with fans

BFI FILM

CLASSICS

the **information** on store

📞01603 773114
email: tis@ccn.ac.uk

21 DAY LOAN ITEM

Please return <u>on or before</u> the last date stamped above

A fine will be charged for overdue items

CITY
COLLEGE
NORWICH

204 308

First published in 2002 by the
BRITISH FILM INSTITUTE
21 Stephen Street, London W1T 1LN

Copyright © Peter Barnes 2002

The British Film Institute
promotes greater understanding
and appreciation of, and
access to, film and moving image
culture in the UK.

British Library Cataloguing-in-Publication Data
A catalogue record for this book is available from the British Library

ISBN 0–85170–919–2

Series design by
Andrew Barron & Collis Clements Associates

Typeset in Fournier and Franklin Gothic by
D R Bungay Associates, Burghfield, Berks

Printed in Great Britain by Cromwell Press, Trowbridge, Wiltshire

CONTENTS

. . . .

NORWICH CITY COLLEGE LIBRARY

204308

791. 4372 WAR BAR

NORWICH CITY COLLEGE
LIBRARY

For Christie and Leela, with my love

Maria Tura (Carole Lombard) and Colonel Ehrhardt (Sig Ruman)

'TO BE OR NOT TO BE'
. . . .

In 1963 during its '100 Clowns' season, Jack Benny came to the National Film Theatre to talk about *To Be or Not to Be*.[1] He told two stories about the film's director, Ernst Lubitsch.

Lubitsch had previously been a successful German silent film actor. On *To Be or Not to Be*, as on all his productions, he acted out every part in every scene before it was shot. According to Benny, he was funny but outrageously over the top. Of course, his cast never told him. In fact they were secretly delighted. Like actors everywhere, they all believed they could play their parts better than their director. He was clear and explicit – more often than not, over-explicit – but gave them great confidence by being so bad. Confidence is the one essential ingredient you must have in playing comedy and Lubitsch gave it to every actor he ever worked with.

Benny also recalled playing a scene and seeing Lubitsch, crouched down beside the camera with a handkerchief stuffed in his mouth to stop himself laughing. Comic business and witticisms (many of them his own) which he must have seen or heard dozens of times before, still sent him into fits of laughter. Benny remembered the incident, after over twenty years, as being the most inspiring in his movie career. He had made a number of films but their directors had never cracked as much as a smile before, during or after production. Maybe that was one of the reasons they are so poor.

The time between when the film was shot in late 1941, and released in 1942, was the very worst of times. In 1941, an unstoppable Hitler had smashed the Allies in the Middle East and was overrunning Russia and besieging Moscow; HMS *Ark Royal* was sunk, Sebastopol fell, Pearl Harbor was bombed and America entered the war, which was going very badly. The Japanese advanced across East Asia, taking Malaya and Singapore, while the Russians were fighting street by street in Leningrad, and thousands were dying daily. In January 1942, Himmler's right hand man, Reihard Heydrich, talked about the extermination of the Jews in the Final Solution and by March Jews were being deported to Auschwitz in Poland. Everything is Poland.

It is important to remember that no-one connected with *To Be or Not to Be* had the gift of prophecy. No-one knew that the Allies would win. In fact, it looked at this stage as if they might lose. This makes the film, among other things, an act of faith and courage, particularly as Lubitsch was one of Hitler's pet hates as an actor. The Nazis were very show-business-orientated, and Hitler had Lubitsch's face plastered on posters at railway stations as an example of a truly degenerate non-Aryan. There really is such a thing as bad publicity.

To produce a comedy about the Nazis' savage occupation of Poland, at a period when the world was engaged in a lethal struggle with rampant fascism, raises questions that are still relevant. For example, are there taboo subjects that cannot be dealt with comedically? Adorno wrote that you cannot write poetry after Auschwitz. What would he have said about writing comedy?

Actually I have personal knowledge of this dilemma. I wrote a theatrical comedy called *Laughter!* about the horrors of Auschwitz Concentration Camp. It asks the question, is laughter, even laughter that freezes in mid air, a legitimate reaction to events too terrible to contemplate, or just a convenient way of making sure we make no effort to stop them happening again? Is laughter truly cathartic or just an excuse to let injustice and oppression exist and do nothing?

More questions. Did Lubitsch and his scriptwriter, Edwin Justus Mayer, really know what was going on in Poland in 1941? Could they have only made a film of such pitch-black humour by being ignorant of the facts? Lubitsch himself answered this point in an article he produced for the *New Yorker* in answer to Bosley Crowther, the paper's dreary, middle-brow film critic, who was wrong on every major film he ever reviewed.

Lubitsch wrote:

> I admit that I have not resorted to the methods usually employed in pictures, novels and plays to signify Nazi terror. No actual torture chamber is photographed, no flogging is shown, no close-up of excited Nazis using whips and rolling their eyes in lust. My Nazis are different: they passed that stage long ago. Brutality, floggings and torture have become their daily routine. They talk about it the same way as a salesman referring to the sale of a handbag. [A reference, perhaps, to Lubitsch's previous film in 1940, *The Shop around the Corner.*] Their humour is built around concentration camps, around the suffering of their victims ...[2]

Lubitsch obviously knew exactly what was going on in Europe in late 1941. By approaching the Nazis in this way he makes them ridiculously evil, instead of heroically evil.

Most tyrants, in and out of uniform, are banal. The absurd President Amin was a monstrous buffoon, Hitler, a blood-soaked Charlie

Chaplin. Franco, Pinochet, Pol Pot, Kissinger, were all smaller and grubbier than legend, with bad teeth and smelly socks. Afterwards we ask how did they get such power and why were they obeyed? The answer is always the same; they got the power because we gave it to them to relieve us of any guilt, and they were obeyed because we wanted to obey them. Monsters are created and exist as convenient scapegoats. Men and women want to do what they do and the monsters provide them with a good excuse. They are blood-stained, sacrificial lambs. Lubitsch wrote to his informal biographer, Herman G. Weinberg in 1947:

> Despite being farcical, *To Be or Not to Be* was a truer picture of Nazism than was shown by most novels, magazine stories and pictures which deal with the same subject. In those, the Germans are pictured as a people who were beleaguered by the Nazi gang and tried to fight the menace through the Underground wherever they could. I never believed in that and I definitely think that this so-called Underground spirit amongst the German people never existed.[3]

It takes a German or an Austrian to know the truth about their respective nations.

To Be or Not to Be also implies that if bone-headed incompetents like Colonel Ehrhardt (Sig Ruman), who regularly escapes from difficulties into disasters, can rise to be a Colonel in the Gestapo, what does this say about the calibre of the rest of the men below and above him? Ehrhardt is a monster but a recognisable monster. He is no Superman, and certainly has no special talents, except for always getting it wrong. He uses fear and lives in fear, sweating in a job too big for him. He is ourselves, dramatised.

Like Otto Preminger and Marlene Dietrich, Lubitsch was never fooled by the Germans. He knew them too well. Preminger told me a story that some time after the end of World War II, he finally forced himself to return to Berlin. The first morning he was walking outside his hotel, and found he kept passing middle-aged men who seemed to recognise him, and almost gave him an automatic 'Hitler' salute. Later he realised that a number of his wartime films, in which he always played Nazi officers, had been finally released in Germany. The befuddled Germans thought he was an old comrade. Preminger had only been doing a job, as a film actor, but the acting – the faking – had become a kind of reality for some of his audiences. His story confirms one of the central ideas of *To Be or Not to Be*

– that it is impossible to separate real life from acting, especially if the acting is bad enough. In other words, it's all show-business.

. . . .

Ernst Lubitsch was born on 28 January 1892, in Berlin, the son of a prosperous tailor. Naturally, all of Lubitsch's characters are immaculately dressed, especially the men. Lubitsch earned an apprenticeship with the famous Max Reinhardt Theatre Company, and made his acting début with them in 1911. It is interesting to note how many distinguished Hollywood directors started with Reinhardt. They included the oddball William Dieterle, director of Buñuel's favourite film, *The Portrait of Jennie* (1948), and the master of stylish American decadence, Douglas Sirk.

From 1914 to 1919, Lubitsch directed and acted in some twenty-seven crude shorts in which he played a greedy shop-boy called Mayer. These shorts are truly terrible; his performance in them is hammy, grating and by today's standards – by any standards – anti-Semitic. There is a complete absence of charm, wit and grace, qualities that were to become the very essence of the mature Lubitsch.

From then on, the only way was up. Lubitsch more or less forsook acting on the screen and confined himself to performing in the rehearsal room. But he always truly loved actors. He made films for them. This is not true of seventy-five per cent of film and theatre directors, who find actors an encumbrance that somehow has to be overlooked or dealt with. Most would prefer hand-puppets, then they could literally claim to do it all.

Lubitsch soon moved into full-time directing, trying everything from expressionist fantasies, romances, farces and comedies, including *The Oyster Princess* (1919) and *I Don't Want to Be a Man* [*Ich Möchte Kein Mann Sein*] (1919). He achieved his biggest success with large-scale, historical epics like *One Arabian Night* [*Sumurun*] (1920) and *Madame Dubarry* (1919).

By the time he left for America in 1923 to direct Mary Pickford in *Rosita* (1923), he had made fourteen features. He never made another picture outside America. Yet, perversely, he almost never made one set in his new-found land. Instead they were set in Lubitschland, a country of charm and sophistication, much like our own, only better, where the thieves, crooks and swindlers – particularly the thieves, crooks and swindlers – had impeccable manners and clean underwear. Lubitschland is a lost continent now, much like Atlantis, but then it never really existed, except in the generous heart of its creator.

In America, he only made romantic comedies and musicals except for a now lost, Tsarist melodrama *The Patriot* (1928) with Emil Jannings and the wan, pacifist piece *The Man I Killed* [*Broken Lullaby*] (1932). This later film was a flop. It is like watching one of Woody Allen's 'serious' films; worthy but depressing, two hours spent grinding your teeth.

I need hardly add that contemporary critics rather liked *The Man I Killed*. It was so relentlessly sincere. One of the problems with it, however, is that it could easily have been a comedy. The absurdist plot, whereby a young man, who has killed Lionel Barrymore's boy, becomes the bereaved man's substitute son, is worthy of one of Lubitsch's intricate farces.

Lubitsch never tried 'serious' again and returned with relief to more frivolous and deeper matters, thereby ensuring he was true to his own greatness and made light of serious subjects like sex and money, love and death.

The director was always surprised that intellectuals treated comedy so dismissively as for those who really know, comedy is much more difficult than tragedy. Comic talent is seldom given as much weight as the merely worthy. This is particularly true of America where playing or writing about a one-eyed, gay, hunchback drug addict is a shoe-in for an Oscar. This is why comics compensate for their low esteem by embarking on totally non-humorous projects to prove their worth. They do not have to: their comedy alone stands as joyous testimony to their importance. After a couple of hiccups, Lubitsch stuck to romantic comedy, realising, perhaps, that people who do nothing but fall in love are more serious and saintly than those who sacrifice their hearts to an idea.

The director was influenced, early on, by Chaplin's *A Woman of Paris* (1923) and some of Cecil B. DeMille's sophisticated comedies like *Don't Change Your Husband* (1918). DeMille and Lubitsch's careers curve in opposite directions. DeMille began by making small, witty comedies and dramas, then changed to lumbering epics, similar to Lubitsch's in Germany, before he switched to comedies of manners.

There is a fascinating production still of DeMille working on *The Sign of the Cross* (1932), surrounded by a massive set and hundreds of extras, and down in one corner are Lubitsch and von Sternberg, who have come on a visit. They are obviously desperately trying to stop giggling at this monstrous display of ostentatious vulgarity.

Some artists change their styles and subject matter repeatedly but a serious artist produces a body of work in which each new piece adds to what has gone before, like an accretion, like coral or a stalactite. There is always a competing stalactite growing alongside. It is the stalactite of popular opinion – what people think of the artist's work. This sometimes overshadows the artist's real achievement and is something he or she can't control.

The director's work in Hollywood from *The Marriage Circle* (1923) to *Trouble in Paradise* (1932), *The Merry Widow* (1934), *The Shop around the Corner* and *Cluny Brown* (1946) has a linking elegance and beauty, which is enhanced, not diminished by time. These so-called frivolous pieces have a resonance and truth that grow more poignant with the years. They are testaments to the best in humanity, to our humour, grace and bravery in the face of life's sad brevity.

For all their speed and humour, Lubitsch's films have a tenderness of heart that is unique in the cinema. Like Renoir's, Lubitsch's characters 'have their reasons'. He doesn't excuse them, but on the other hand, he doesn't moralise. This is one of the differences between him and his film disciple, Billy Wilder, who usually sits in judgment and deals out appropriate punishments to his nefarious characters. Poor, delightful Walter Neff in *Double Indemnity* (1944) gets the electric chair and the down-at-heel journalist in *Ace in the Hole* (1951) gets a pair of scissors in his stomach.

Lubitsch gives the thieves in *Trouble in Paradise*, the philandering husband in *Heaven Can Wait* (1943) and the shady ladies of *Angel* (1937) a wry smile. He never passes sentence, being too busy enjoying their absurd, but understandable desire to have it all; to break the rules and not pay the bill for there is always a bill to pay, and Lubitsch discreetly pays it himself and lets his scallywags slide away to face another day. He forgives them because they have style and mystery and an all-saving humour. Above all they never lack a bracing appreciation of the ridiculous.

For a glimpse of the richness of Lubitsch's treasure trove of memorable scenes, I will just point to two favourites, chosen at random. The first is from *One Hour with You* (1932) between two minor characters. Andre (Charles Ruggles), the dyspeptic suitor of the heroine, Colette (Jeannette MacDonald), is dressed as Romeo, in tights and ruffles. He talks to Colette on the phone and finds the party he is going to isn't fancy dress … 'What? What? … not a costume party?' He calls his valet and tells him the news. The valet replies 'Ah, Monsieur, I did so want to see you in tights.' We hold on Andre's face, blank and baffled. He blinks rapidly, only his eyes betraying a sudden panic.

The other episode is from *If I Had a Million* (1932), an anthology of short stories about people who receive a million dollars by chance.

Lubitsch directed the shortest episode, *The Clerk*. It lasts two minutes eighteen seconds and consists of exactly twelve shots. Phineas V. Lambert (Charles Laughton) is an accountant in a large room with rows of identical desks. He is writing in a ledger when a messenger drops a letter on his desk which contains the million dollar cheque. Laughton sweeps it aside, without looking up, as he finishes making an entry in his account book. The movement itself is sublime, one of the most defining gestures on film. Just as Godard pointed out Debbie Reynolds instinctively pulling down her skirt at the end of the 'Good Morning' number in *Singin' in the Rain* (1952) as she somersaults over the back of the sofa, encapsulates forever an unspoilt, radiant innocence, so Laughton's sweep suggest an action that has been repeated endlessly on hundreds of different letters dropped on his desk. He has been so conditioned that he acts like a machine; he is not a man but a 'clerk'. The gesture suggests a lifetime of mechanical efficiency and human emptiness. And yet this impatient sweep of the hand is physically beautiful. It has a grace that belies its setting and its meaning. It is pure cinema for it tells us unspoken things – in this case contradictory things. People can be defined just by their physical actions. Film at its best can be very moral. It shows us we must be suspicious of what people say – they'll say anything – but watch what they do: the real truth is in the body language. Joseph Conrad said that he wanted to make people *see*. Cinema does that.

After knocking the letter aside, Laughton opens it, flattens it out and reads it, and the cheque. There is no reaction. He just gets up and we see him making his way to the president's office, first going up a flight of steps, then, in four shots, going through four different doors from 'Administrative Offices', 'Secretary to the President', 'The Private Secretary to the President', and to the simple, but inspiring, 'Mr Brown, President', as befits the president of the company.

As Mr Brown sits behind an ornate desk, reading through some papers, Laughton comes in and gives him a massively ripe raspberry.

Lubitsch provided a different final shot for Britain. Instead of blowing a raspberry, Laughton gives an 'up-yours' V-sign with his fingers while making a rude noise with his mouth. Either way, the revolution has come. The meek, oppressed, middle-class clerk of legend has finally rebelled. We, the audience, explode with satisfied laughter. Freedom at last! We overlook the sad moral: you have to have money to be free.

. . . .

To Be or Not to Be has a simple basic premise and a fiendishly intricate plot which is like a series of Chinese boxes. In essence, a group of Polish actors (mostly Jewish) impersonate Gestapo officers in order to save themselves and the Polish Underground.

Actually the plot, if played straight and not for laughs, could be an episode from the long-running 1960 American TV series, *Mission Impossible*, which involved ludicrously impossible plots and deception, perpetrated by a team of American spies, battling the non-American forces of evil – mostly Communists and drug lords. These heroes were masters of disguise and always played different roles, to defeat their enemies. Unlike the characters in *To Be or Not to Be* they were unaware how ludicrous it all was. Although the splendid Martin Landau, it has to be said, could easily have joined Joseph Tura's Polish acting troupe.

It is important to outline the story of *To Be or Not to Be* in some detail. The formal Swiss-watch plotting is part of the fun as we watch every detail pay off, even down to an actor's false moustache.

In 1939 Hitler appears, all by himself, walking down a Warsaw street. As a crowd gathers, a sonorous narrator asks how could this possibly be? 'It must be true! No doubt! The man with the little moustache … Adolf Hitler! Adolf Hitler in Warsaw … '

The scene shifts to Gestapo headquarters where a group of preening Gestapo officers, led by Colonel Ehrhardt, are bribing a small boy with a toy to betray his parents. They have been spreading a lame joke about the Führer. 'They named a brandy after Napoleon, and they made a herring out of Bismarck, and Hitler is going to end up as …' A subordinate gives the punchline *'A piece of cheese!'* When he sees the others aren't laughing, he is terrified. The same joke is repeated later in the film by the real Colonel Ehrhardt who is even more terrified when he realises no-one is laughing either.

But nothing is what it seems in the film. Illusion and reality are deliberately blurred. The Gestapo headquarters are, in fact, a stage set and the Gestapo officers are actors. We are on the stage of the Polski Theatre in the middle of a rehearsal of a new anti-Nazi play. A character actor, Bronski, who is playing Hitler, has gone into the streets of Warsaw to test the effectiveness of his make-up and performance. It seems fine, until a child comes up to him and asks for his autograph. Bronski is disturbed, he has been unmasked, but still signs, flattered he has been recognised.

The actors argue about their performances. The director objects when the leading lady, Maria Tura, wants to appear in a scene in a

'Hitler' in Warsaw

The 'Gestapo' bribe a boy to betray his parents

concentration camp in a stunning evening dress and is shocked by the accusation of bad taste. She is defended by her husband, 'that great, great Polish actor' Joseph Tura. It could be said of him that he will remain an actor to the end of his days, and die in his own arms.

Everything stops when an official, frightened of offending Germany, bans the play. The company replaces the new play with *Hamlet*.

Maria begins a flirtation with a handsome pilot, Lieutenant Sobinski. She meets him in her dressing room when her husband begins his *Hamlet* soliloquy, 'To be or not to be'. Taking Maria's responses as real and not understanding she is always acting, Sobinski wants to tell her husband about their relationship. Maria is appalled. 'Fortunately' at that moment, the Germans invade Poland. Tura doesn't react to the news; he is still in a state of shock that someone walked out in the middle of his soliloquy. Poland is being invaded but Tura is more concerned with his reception. It is a matter of getting things in perspective.

Sobinski escapes to England where he becomes a member of the Polish Squadron of the Royal Air Force. An apparent Polish patriot, Professor Siletsky, gets the names of the pilots' relatives, still living in Poland.

The real Hitler greets his troops

Sobinski realises the professor must be a German spy when he doesn't know who the famous Maria Tura is. But Professor Siletsky has left for Warsaw. Sobinski is ordered to get there ahead of him and kill him before he can give the list of names to the Gestapo.

Once in Warsaw, he contacts the Underground through Maria. Her husband, though deeply suspicious of Sobinski, agrees to help. The theatrical company conceive an elaborate plot in which Maria Tura pretends to be attracted to Professor Siletsky who is lured into the Polski Theatre, now transformed into Gestapo headquarters. Joseph Tura impersonates the Gestapo chief, Colonel Ehrhardt, in order to get Professor Siletsky's list of names. Siletsky eventually becomes suspicious, mainly because Tura runs out of improvised lines. Professor Siletsky tries to escape but is killed onstage.

The plot then turns inside out as Tura now disguises himself as Professor Siletsky in order to meet the real Colonel Ehrhardt, who turns out to be a monstrous, bug-eyed buffoon, the Pere Ubu of the SS. All goes well until the body of the real Professor Siletsky is found. Tura saves himself by convincing Ehrhardt the dead Siletsky is a fake. His fellow actors appear, led by Rawitch and reveal the live Siletsky is a fake and drag him away to the utter bewilderment of the colonel.

Tura and his fellow actors are now in great danger but pull off a brilliant coup by infiltrating, as Gestapo officers, a gala performance, held in the Polski Theatre, in honour of Hitler himself. Bronski finally gets to play his Hitler for real, while another spear-carrier, Greenberg performs 'Shylock' in the corridor for the Nazi party hacks.

The troupe escape to England in Hitler's plane and resume their acting careers. The last we see of them is Tura as Hamlet, beginning his 'To be or not to be' soliloquy, while beadily watching Sobinski in the audience. The lieutenant stays in his seat, but another handsome young officer gets up instead, to make his way to Maria's dressing room.

. . . .

To Be or Not to Be has one of the most distinguished sets of credits in movies. You must work with the best to get the best work. Lubitsch was never afraid to surround himself with brilliant talents. Look at the list. Co-producer, the flamboyant Alexander Korda; the Designer, Vincent Korda, Alex's more brilliant brother: Music, Werner R. Heymann; Camera, the great cameraman, Rudolph Maté; Story, Lubitsch and Melchior Lengyel; Actors, Jack Benny, Carole Lombard, Sig Ruman, Robert Stack, and way down at the bottom of the cast list, as Scottish

Farmer, James Finlayson, the immortal antagonist of so many Laurel and Hardy films. The scriptwriter was Edwin Justus Mayer.

In writing this appreciation, I read many reviews and other accounts of *To Be or Not to Be*. In ninety per cent of them, the screenwriter was not even mentioned. The film, it seems, wrote itself or sprang, Minerva-like, from the head of Lubitsch alone. Critics know nothing about screenwriting and care even less; Lubitsch knew better.

Lubitsch believed the script was the very bedrock of the film. It was the bible. 'Once the script is written,' Lubitsch said, 'I've finished the picture. All I have to do is photograph it. As you write the script, you cut the film, you build the sets, you light your players, you design your wardrobe, you set the tempo, you delineate the characters … For me, it is virtually done in the script.'

Lubitsch worked on all his scripts and committed them to memory so he had no need to refer to them during shooting. Of course this is reminiscent of Hitchcock. He, however, resented actually shooting the picture, after having shot it perfectly in his head. Lubitsch loved the process. He was always an actor; Hitchcock was always an editor.

To Be or Not to Be was the only film on which Lubitsch always claimed a credit (but not on screen), though his involvement in all his previous films at the writing stage was overwhelming and crucial. In this one, he worked on the story with Melchior Lengyel who said, 'Writing with Lubitsch was just kibitzing.'[4] We must take him at his word. Lubitsch, like Feydeau, needed another person in the room when he was writing, to bounce ideas off. It could be anyone, as long as they were friends. Feydeau had dozens of collaborators who went on to do nothing, without the great farceur.

The story itself is pure Ernst Lubitsch; stylish, witty, fiendishly ingenious, but the screenplay is pure Edwin Justus Mayer. He had worked on the script of a previous, Lubitsch-produced film, *Desire* (1936), with Waldemar Young and Samuel Hoffenstein.

Mayer was different from any of the screenwriters Lubitsch had worked with before. *To Be or Not to Be* has a comic seriousness, a hard-edged, mordant savagery, which is unique for this director. His favourite screenwriter, the brilliant, urbane Samson Raphaelson, had turned down the assignment, fortunately. With all his special gifts, Raphaelson would have been wrong. He did not have the touch of the abyss in him which black comedy needs to be wholly successful. Raphaelson's work has a priceless wit, sublime airiness and sly humour but it would not have fitted in the world of Colonel Ehrhardt. There is a deliberate shallowness in Raphaelson's work. The viewer, sometimes, comes away from his films feeling he found working in the movies slightly distasteful and his plays like *The Jazz Singer* were more important and more personal.

In the end, Mayer was the best writer Lubitsch ever worked with, and he worked with some of the best. The actual mechanics of the plot were as intricate as the best of Raphaelson. Look at the way a prop like Tura's non-adhesive moustache is used, again and again. It lands Tura in trouble at Gestapo headquarters, which he gets out of brilliantly. But it is later responsible for Colonel Ehrhardt's ludicrous suicide. Mayer's jokes are the equal of Billy Wilder's, but less glib, more deeply felt, and therefore more shocking and funny. He has an intellectual toughness, a bracing wit which isn't afraid to go the whole way; he hasn't Wilder's ultimate soft centre.

....

In the 1920s, Edwin Justus Mayer had a hit play, *The Firebrand*, on Broadway, starring Frank Morgan as the Florentine artist, Cellini. It was later turned into a musical, scored by Kurt Weill, with lyrics by Ira Gershwin. The play is amusing but empty. His second play, *Children of Darkness* (1928) was a failure but a minor masterpiece. It possesses all the comic qualities of *To Be or Not to Be*, or rather, the film possesses all the best qualities of the play, which is set in eighteenth-century Newgate Prison where a group of prisoners are either being incarcerated indefinitely or awaiting execution. If they can pay for the privilege, they are reasonably housed but like the trio in Sartre's *Huis Clos*, they have nothing to do but cheat and double-cross each other and wait for a non-existent reprieve or a hanging.

MR SNAP: Pray, my lord, may I enquire for what you are held?
LORD WAINWRIGHT: (indifferently) I poisoned my wife – and a few of her intimate friends.
MR SNAP: Dear me! Why did you do that?
LORD WAINWRIGHT: A gentleman does not discuss his family affairs with a vulgar stranger.
MR SNAP: Gentleman! 'Tis true – you seem such a gentleman.
LORD WAINWRIGHT: I am a lord, Mr Snap and would have you know that all eminent poisoners were of good family; 'twas a symptom of their subtle breeding. You will do me the justice of not

derogating my rank because I rid the world of a few useless people; a fact which, in any competent civilisation, would indubitably raise my rank.[5]

In the first production of *Children of Darkness* in New York, one of the producers was Kenneth Macgowan who later had a very distinguished career as a Hollywood producer, working with Fritz Lang and Hitchcock. The play ran for seventy-nine performances on Broadway in the same season as Preston Sturges' *Strictly Dishonorable* and the Gershwins' *Strike up the Band*. It was dismissed as too depressing for the Depression. It's true, Mayer's timing was off in presenting this steely, tragic comedy at such a moment. Its black humour and stylish brilliance would make it an anomaly at the best of times in the American theatre which, then as now, was awash with sentimental naturalism. *Children of Darkness* is like a lost Restoration play, edged with terror.

I trawled through numerous encyclopaedias of American drama and there was little or no mention of Edwin Justus Mayer, though Louis B. Mayer had a surprising paragraph in one, and quantities of words were consumed on second stringers like Lillian Hellman.

My reading of encyclopaedias was not totally wasted, however, as I came across fascinating bits of information. That John (Jules) Garfield appeared in a musical comedy about the Borsht Belt called *Wish You Were Here* (1937) with the great film gangster Sheldon Leonard (*Guys and Dolls*, 1955), playing a character called Pinkie Aaronson; that Walter Huston started in vaudeville with his second wife, Bayone Whipple, and his first big hit was playing Elmer Kane, the moronic, brain-dead pitcher in Ring Lardner's *Elmer the Great* (1933); that Florence Bates, the monumental, tippling ballet teacher in *On the Town* (1949) started her career as a charming little girl in the first production of the famous *Peck's Bad Boys*; that Olsen of Olsen and Johnson was Peruvian.

There was one item about Mayer in *The Oxford Companion To American Theatre*.[6] Set out the flags. It said he was a native of New York, a newspaper man for many years, then briefly an actor, that the original production of *Children of Darkness* was a failure but a 1958 revival in the Circle in the Square Theatre in New York was a success and forced a re-evaluation of the play. I have to confess, I have seen no sign of such a re-evaluation. The item ends with the chilling words: 'He was long active as a screenwriter.' Recognition for good work is rarely heard in America – or anywhere for that matter – even when you are dead, and especially if you have not been commercially successful.

In the first American cast of the play, the principal female lead, Laetitia, was taken by an English actress and former singer who had once partnered Chaliapin: Mary Ellis. She was the original Rose Marie and the wife in the first production of Rattigan's *The Browning Version*. All things connect. I worked with Ms Ellis on a radio play in 1982, when she was in her eighties. She was astonished when I mentioned *Children of Darkness* as she thought no-one had heard of the play. Surprisingly, she remembered it as great theatre and could not understand why its author had not gone on to have a brilliant theatrical career. She couldn't remember anything else about the production because she was determined not to look back on her faded theatre clippings. She was more interested in the novel she was writing, which was subsequently published to great acclaim. I hope I grow old with such eternal enthusiasm and grace.

Perhaps the reason why Mayer never developed into a major dramatist has more to do with the culture of success hanging heavy in the American air. Only the bloody-minded Eugene O'Neill made himself immune.

Mayer apparently hated Hollywood though[7] – or should it be 'because'? – he wrote consistently for all the major studios during the 1930s and 1940s. He was born 8 November 1896 in New York, and died 11 September 1960, having gone to Hollywood in the late 1920s. As far as one can discover he never went back to the theatre. He worked on silent films and ended up writing in various capacities on some forty movies. Among the dim highlights would be *Desire* which Frank Borzage directed and Dorothy Arzner's *Merrily We Go to Hell* (1932). He worked on *Gone with the Wind* (1939) for $4,167 which gives us one reason why he stayed in Hollywood. He could not afford to leave. His chains were golden.

None of the films showed any glimpse of his talent except *Midnight* (1939) for which he wrote the original story. It was scripted by Wilder and Brackett and remains one of the best screwball comedies for three-quarters of its length.

The rest is well-paid hack work which is only excusable for a writer of his talent if the writer uses money earned to subsidise his true métier like Faulkner, Fitzgerald and Isherwood. Mayer did not. Instead he whinged and wasted the money on living in style. No life ever ends up being the one originally scripted, and with time, it seems, all lives go to waste. Mayer, however, was given the opportunity, near the end, to write a screenplay that was the equal of *Children of Darkness*.

In movies, he struck it lucky once. With Lubitsch he had a director who considered the script everything. He always worked closely with the writer and their first script was always the only script. Samuel Raphaelson has a very touching memory of working with the man.

> Lubitsch did need a writer but he wasn't afraid of a good writer, which Hitchcock, I suspect, was, for very complex and obscure reasons. Lubitsch welcomed a good writer. That man had a sense of good writing second to none. If Shakespeare had been alive at his time, Lubitsch would have happily embraced him. And Shakespeare would have been a little better than he was … Lubitsch never cheapened you.[8]

Uniquely, for Lubitsch, *To Be or Not to Be* has an entirely original script. For twenty years, all his films were based on obscure European plays, usually Hungarian. 'Because,' according to Raphaelson, 'you could have a play that fell apart and still have a success in Budapest.' I believe you still can.

Edwin Justus Mayer has one enduring play and one enduring film to his credit. Not enough, perhaps. On the other hand, it is an achievement. Other, equally talented writers have much less to show for a lifetime spent in the salt-mines of Hollywood, or the moral quagmire of Broadway.

. . . .

It is salutary to think that many reading this book will not know who Jack Benny was. The choreographer George Balanchine once said: 'Publicity over-rates everything. Picasso's over-rated. I'm over-rated. Even Jack Benny's over-rated.'[9] Actually he never was but he made few films and most of them were poor. He flowered in radio, television and on the stage, where his work is the equal of Laurel and Hardy, W. C. Fields, Keaton, Mae West, Jerry Lewis and Will Hay.

But because he was not a film comedian, he is easily forgotten. You can savour his work on radio tapes and TV videos, but there is no major film except *To Be or Not to Be* and a magnificent cameo performance in *It's in the Bag* [*The Fifth Chair*] (1945), where he locks horns with fellow comic, Fred Allen, in an acid sketch which ends with Allen admiring Benny's tie and Benny taking it off, gift-wrapping it and with his personal cash register ringing merrily, selling it to him for a few dollars.

Benny's comic persona, which was created in the beginning by a brilliant gag-writer, A. L. Boasberg,[10] was made up in equal parts of meanness and vanity. Just as Bob Hope had cowardice, another Boasberg creation, Benny had legendary meanness, and it was used to great comic effect. In this he was a quintessential American. He loved a dollar more than life and was the living comic symbol of rampant capitalism. In a famous radio show, Benny walks along a deserted street, late at night. He is held up by a mugger.

> MUGGER: Don't make a move, this is a stick up!
> BENNY: What?
> MUGGER: You heard me. Your money or your life.
> BENNY: Mister ... mister, put down that gun.
> MUGGER: Shut up ... now come on ... your money or your life ...

There is an infinitely long pause.

> MUGGER: Look bud, I said, 'Your money or your life.'
> BENNY: Hhmmm ... I'm thinking it over.[11]

Lubitsch does not use Benny's meanness in his film. But he does use his comic vanity.

Jack Benny about to sell his tie to Fred Allen, *It's in the Bag*

In Benny's ongoing radio feud with Fred Allen, the two monumental egos continually clash. It is interesting to think of Allen playing the part of Joseph Tura – sour, downbeat and totally disillusioned. It would have been funny but would you have believed he would ever have worked for the Polish Resistance?[12]

Lubitsch always had Benny in mind for the lead when the script was being written. The comedian's career in films up to this point, despite the commercial success of *George Washington Slept Here*, had been dismal. So it was natural for Benny to ask Lubitsch why he wanted him for the part. 'I'm a comedian,' he said, 'not an actor. Why do you want me for this picture?'

Lubitsch replied 'You think you're a comedian. You're not a comedian. You're not even a clown, who is a performer what is doing funny things. A comedian – he is a performer what is saying funny things. But you, Jack, you're an actor, you're an actor playing the part of a comedian and this you are doing very well. But do not worry, I keep your secret to myself.'[13] This secret is the reason why Benny is the ideal Tura, an actor who is playing the part of a Resistance leader and German spy and 'doing very well'.

Benny rarely told jokes on stage, television and particularly radio: he used silences, 'slow burns' and pregnant 'hmms' to get laughs. It shows what confidence Benny had in Lubitsch – and Lubitsch had in himself – that he allows the director to deprive him of a large part of his comic persona – his legendary meanness, his all-consuming love of the almighty dollar.

Benny's vanity over his looks, age and violin playing is displaced into Joseph Tura's vanity as a 'great, great actor'. He is comfortable because his paranoia is matched by that of his wife, Maria, and the rest of the acting company. It is also shared by his Nazi adversaries. It is difficult to imagine Colonel Ehrhardt sleeping easily. Instead of counting sheep, he would be counting the mistakes he had made the previous day and calculating who was to blame. Even the long-suffering Schultz, despite his stoic demeanour, can never rest easy, knowing he is the perennial scapegoat for every botch-up made by his superior. The fact that these two are Nazis does not alter the fact that their relationship and characters are reproduced every morning in offices all over the world.

In his radio and television shows Benny is always the butt of other people's jokes. But he is still the head of the team. Just as Joseph Tura is the undisputed star of the Polish troupe. Despite Colonel Ehrhardt's devastating Shakespearean put-down ('what he did to Shakespeare we are

Tura sees someone get up to leave

doing now to Poland'), Tura's self-confidence is never really shattered, even when a man walks out during his soliloquy. He consoles himself with the thought that the man may have suffered a tragic loss and had to leave. The only thing that could disrupt Tura's self-confidence is losing Maria, and that could never happen; they are too much in love with each other and themselves.

The comedian confessed that *To Be or Not to Be* was his best film – perhaps his only film and his performance remains sublime. When *To Be or Not to Be* played in a cinema in Miami Beach, Benny's aged father paid a visit. After seeing his son appear in the opening scene as a Nazi officer, Benny Sr grabbed his nurse's arm and stamped out of the theatre. He could not believe his son had given a Nazi salute. Benny told his father 'Go back and see it. I'm against the Nazis. I'm fighting them. Go back and see it all the way through.'[14] His father did and completely changed his opinion. In this he showed a tolerance and open-mindedness singularly missing from film critics of the period.

. . . .

The casting of classic American movies always, in the end, turns out to be a matter of luck. Look who we could have ended up with in *Casablanca*

(1942) or *The Maltese Falcon* (1941) – Ronald Reagan and George Raft as the respective leads.

Miriam Hopkins was originally cast as Maria Tura but when she read the script she found she was not the star. She tried to persuade Lubitsch and Benny to make her part bigger. When they refused, she quit.

Hopkins' work for Lubitsch in *Design for Living* and particularly *Trouble in Paradise* is exemplary; she is funny and vulnerable and sexy. Her professional crook, Lily, in *Trouble in Paradise* is a free woman, worldly, resourceful, but not too cynical; a companion any man would be proud to have. But Hopkins did not realise no other director but Lubitsch could bring out those qualities in her. She needed *To Be or Not to Be* but one feels she never got past counting the lines of the script, something Benny could have warned her about.

On the other hand, Carole Lombard, who took the part, desperately wanted to work with Lubitsch. Benny allowed her top billing as he had the top part. She told her biographer that the film was the happiest of her career: 'The one time when everything began right, stayed right and ended right.'[15] And it shows in her performance; a razor-sharp intelligence working at maximum capacity.

By the time filming was completed in December 1941, America was in World War II. Three weeks later, Lombard herself was killed, with her mother, in a plane crash on a tour selling war bonds. There was national grief over her loss, which did not help *To Be or Not to Be* where she plays a glamorous, but not obviously sympathetic actress, who may be cheating on her husband with a young airman.

Her early death after making her best film, makes the loss more poignant, but fixes her grace and beauty forever. We will never see her as a middle-aged character actress so our image of her is at her best. It is as if Barbara Stanwyck finished on the high of *Double Indemnity*, Jean Arthur in *The More the Merrier* (1943), Ginger Rogers in *Roxie Hart* (1942).

What marks out Lombard is not only her beauty and intelligence, but also her comic speed and timing. She packs more into a line, or between a line, than any film actress before or since. But there is another quality special to her. On screen she often looks as though she is dreaming. Though her intelligence is jet-fuelled, there is an almost 'swimming underwater' quality about her persona. What is she dreaming of? Possibly another life, another character, another world.

This quality makes her work in flawed movies like George Stevens' *Vigil in the Night* (1939) as a masochistically dedicated nurse extraordinarily powerful. Her firecracker performance in *Twentieth Century* (1934) matches John Barrymore blow for blow. She brought a splendid dream quality to the dim-witted heroine of *My Man Godfrey* (1936). Most of her movies are unavailable today. Many sound intriguing and one would particularly like to catch *The Young Bride* (1934) in which she plays a chorus girl who marries a series of gangsters for their money and short lives. In all her films she had that quality which cannot be learned – charm, true charm not fake, not laid-on, not manufactured.

The speed of her reaction to situations, comic or dramatic, make most film actresses, particularly contemporary actresses, look laboured. Her 'curving' and timing of comic dialogue is unique.

Look at her marvellous reading of the following speech:

> MARIA: Whenever there is a chance to take the spotlight away from me ... it's becoming ridiculous, the way you grab attention. Whenever I start to tell a story, you finish it ... if I go on a diet, you lose weight ... if I have a cold, you cough ... and if I should have a baby, I'm not so sure I'd be the mother.
> TURA: I'm satisfied to be the father.

Carole Lombard goes domestic with ex-husband William Powell in *My Man Godfrey*

Lombard rattles through this dialogue on a note of rising indignation and at breakneck speed, particularly the sentence beginning 'Whenever I start …'. This contains three jokes about storytelling, dieting and coughing. Lombard deliberately throws them away in order to hit the last joke at the end 'and if I should have a baby, I'm not so sure I'd be the mother'. If she had slowed down to get the previous three small laughs, it would have taken away from the big one, which was where it should be, at the end. Her indignation is punctured and laugh capped by Benny's deflating line 'I'm satisfied to be the father'.

Lubitsch, of course, could have directed her to say her lines this way, but there is enough evidence in her previous comedies to show she instinctively knew at what pace comedy dialogue should be delivered. The director told David Niven that 'to play comedy you had to have a circus inside you'. Lombard certainly had one inside her and the show was always on.[16]

Tura has just come off stage, and orders refreshments on the internal phone. 'Hello, this is Mr Tura. Will you please order me a salami and cheese sandwich and a glass of beer? … right away, please. Thank you … ' Maria swans past.

> TURA: The audience is a little cool tonight.
> MARIA: Not to me.

Her look is ethereal, her voice lilting, her timing lethal. In another scene Maria is giving Tura unconvincing explanations of why a Polish pilot is walking out during Tura's soliloquy, 'To be or not to be'. The truth is he is going to see her in her dressing room.

> TURA: Oh he's just one of those poor boys who hasn't the price of a ticket, but inherited a lot of flowers, and is trying to get rid of them. Three nights in a row! Even Shakespeare couldn't stand seeing *Hamlet* three nights in succession.
> MARIA: You forget you are playing Hamlet.
> TURA: Oh, that's right.

Her line is played with such wide-eyed sincerity, with not the faintest trace of cynicism that Tura's paranoia is suddenly brought to a grinding halt as he realises it is blindingly obvious the only reason anyone would come to *Hamlet* three nights in a row is to see his performance.

Sobinski proposes marriage to Maria in her dressing room

Maria meets Professor Siletsky, who tries to persuade her to become a spy for the Germans.

SILETSKY: Why don't you stay here for dinner? I can imagine nothing more charming and before the evening is over I'm sure you will say 'Heil Hitler'.

MARIA: I would like to accept your invitation, but just as you want to represent the Nazi case in the very best light, I would like to represent the Polish case in a more suitable dress.

SILETSKY: I understand perfectly but please don't let me wait too long.

MARIA: Au revoir.

SILETSKY: Just a moment. I'm looking forward to it.

MARIA: So am I.

SILETSKY: This lady is permitted to leave.

GUARD: Yes, sir.

SILETSKY: This is a very difficult place to get in but it is much more difficult to get out.

MARIA: Oh, I am terribly frightened and terribly thrilled. Bye!

'I am terribly frightened and terribly thrilled. Bye!'

Listen to her breathless, sexy rendering of 'terribly frightened' and subtle accentuation of 'thrilled' to be topped by a lingering 'Bye'. The reading is inventive, individual and utterly convincing. The audience know she is lying but within the film Siletsky would be convinced she *is* actually frightened and thrilled. She is doing two things in the reading; lying and being true to the character – after all, she is playing an actress, acting. She is inside as well as outside the character, never for a moment succumbing to the temptation to dive too deep and never surface. Brecht would have adored her. She is able to tell an audience the author's intentions without stepping out of character. It's a gift.

Scott Fitzgerald famously said 'The rich are different from us'. I wonder if the line should have been 'The beautiful are different from us'. Lombard was breathtakingly beautiful and maybe she was different, living in a different world, which she came out of from time to time.

She had style of course. But I do not know if that gets us very far. Is style 'grace under pressure'? I never know what that means. It cannot just mean elegance in an inelegant situation, nor can it just mean a certain kind of courage in facing the world. Style has no morals. Cowards can have it; look at Hamlet. Talking of courage, Lubitsch had it too. Only a brave man would have set *To Be or Not to Be* – a Jewish show with Jewish performers, playing Jewish actors – in Poland, the most anti-Semitic country in Europe.

To see Lombard and Benny together is like watching two great professional tennis players at the top of their game, with the ball swerving, dipping, spinning and slicing over the net, without either one of them ever losing their exquisite stroke or timing. Lombard was called the queen of screwball comedy although she came to the genre late in her career, in the 1930s, having started in silent movies.

Her best work lies in films like *True Confessions* (1937) where she plays a compulsive liar who is only saved from being convicted of murder by luck. She alone saves *My Man Godfrey* from being a cop-out Depression comedy. She gives an unsentimental emotional depth (not in the script or direction) to Hazel Flagg, the 'heroic' radium victim of *Nothing Sacred* (1937).

The director Wesley Ruggles who made three pictures with her said 'she plays straight but uses comedy techniques', while Hawks remembered her as 'a marvellous girl. Crazy as a bed bug.'[17] But let Lombard have the last word. She said of herself: 'I loved Hollywood, tried having a good time, particularly men – weeee!'[18]

. . . .

Many marvellous Hollywood character actors from the halcyon 1930s and 1940s are given a chance to spread their wings in *To Be or Not to Be*. There is the expressive, sad-faced comedy actor of hundreds of movies, Tom Dugan (Bronski/Hitler), including the New York cop from *On the Town* (1949) who is appalled when he hears that a dinosaur exhibit has been wrecked in a New York museum. He is stunned because he mistakenly believes it is his favourite singer, Dinah Shore, who has been wrecked.

In *To Be or Not to Be* he is Bronski, the perennial spear-carrier. He and his friend Greenberg (Felix Bressart) have been carrying spears onstage for years and will continue to do so without getting the chance to play major roles. Bronski does get to play Hitler but even that ends disappointingly when the play is cancelled. But even before that, Bronski's talent is slighted by the director, Dobosh (Charles Halton), who stops rehearsal of the play when Bronski marches on dressed as Hitler.

DOBOSH: I don't know. It's not convincing. To me he's just a man with a little moustache.
MAKE-UP MAN: But so is Hitler.

DOBOSH: No, no, no … wait, it's not just the moustache, it's something … I don't know, well I just can't smell Hitler in him.
GREENBERG: I can.

Dobosh finally points to a large, framed blow-up picture of Hitler on the set wall.

DOBOSH: That picture, that's what he should look like!
BRONSKI: But that picture was taken of me.
DOBOSH: Then the picture is wrong too.

Which is why Bronski goes into the streets of Warsaw to prove his point. Perhaps Dugan could play Bronski with such humour and truth because he had long been a perennial spear-carrier in an endless succession of American movies.

His genuine awe of his friend and fellow carrier Greenberg's rendering of Shylock's speech 'Do I not have eyes' is touching. There is a beautiful little scene between the two friends when they are out of work, shovelling snow, and lamenting the fact that they are no longer carrying spears, only shovels.

I was, at one stage, uneasy about Felix Bressart's performance as the lowly actor, Greenberg. It seemed to me to hover on the edge of sentimentality and I thought, perhaps, it toppled over. It does not. The self-pity in the playing is comic and disciplined. Greenberg is a spear-carrier who is self-pitying because he wants to play Shylock and knows he will never be given the chance. But he finally gets his wish.

We see him during the course of the film, give three different readings of the Shylock speech, 'Do I not have eyes …'. Each reading is subtly different. His final reading is 'for real' when he has to distract a group of Nazi officers. It is quavering, tearful, pathetic, just the sort of reading Greenberg would give after having waited years for the chance. He has forgotten the danger and is relishing every minute of his performance.

So Greenberg gets to play Shylock just as his fellow spear-carrier, Bronski, gets to play Hitler 'for real' and they both pull it off marvellously. The fact that both their performances are over the top, and that none of the Nazis notice is part of the joke. Lubitsch – like God – tried to give his characters their hearts' desire, if he could, even if they did not get it in quite the way they expected.

Lionel Atwill is the magnificent ham, Rawitch, who, when pretending to be a German general, still looks and acts like he

The spear-carriers shovelling snow

'Do I not have eyes …'

could step into a touring production of *The Desert Song* at a moment's notice.

Again, an actor of vast experience in movies, he was, at least, given a chance to play leads. In Joseph von Sternberg's *The Devil Is a Woman* (1935) he is even a surrogate for the director himself. He plays a morose victim of frustration and folly, forever being teased and tantalised by Marlene Dietrich's *femme fatale*. Though the film itself glides into giggling campness, Atwill's performance is very powerful. His 'hero' is an absurd but not ridiculous figure. He plays an idiot but not idiotically, just as he does in *To Be or Not to Be*.

His Rawitch booms his way in and out of every scene but it is played from the inside. Rawitch never sees himself as we see him.

In a wonderful theatrical touch, he is backstage, dressed as Claudius, doing warm-up vocal exercises. As he walks down the corridor humming and gargling to himself, the royal crown on his head hits an overhead metal lightshade. It makes a distinct clang. But Rawitch walks on, still doing his vocal exercises, blissfully unaware. He has not been made ridiculous because he hasn't noticed or heard the clang. He is too busy preparing for the show.

When Professor Siletsky is taken to see the fake Colonel Ehrhardt, he is ushered into a supposed office at Gestapo headquarters, manned by the Polski Theatre company as Gestapo officers. Rawitch pretends to come out of Colonel Ehrhardt's inner office.

> RAWITCH: Goodbye Colonel. [he laughs] … Heil Hitler.
> SILETSKY: Heil Hitler.
> RAWITCH: Why isn't this the gentleman from England, Captain Mumm?
> ACTOR/ADJUTANT: Yes, Colonel.
> RAWITCH: It's a great pleasure to meet you, Professor. A very great pleasure. [laughs] Well, you certainly fooled the English didn't you? [laughs] 'The British Lion will drink his tea from saucers made in Germany' [laughs]. Huh? … Heil Hitler.

He finally leaves. What adds to the hilarity of this scene is that the actor playing Captain Mumm (George Lynn) has been standing behind Professor Siletsky, miming frantically for Rawitch to stop talking and get out. The fact is Rawitch repeatedly looks as though he is about to leave but continues to stand by the open door, embellishing his exit lines. Exit

Rawitch: 'The British Lion will drink his tea from saucers made in Germany'

lines are always important for actors, they might never get back into the play, so it is vital they make a lasting impression.

Rawitch is desperately improvising gobbledegook. Where does the line 'The British Lion will drink his tea from saucers made in Germany' come from? What does it mean? Rawitch can't think of anything to say so says anything. It is a speech uttered in complete desperation, which is why it is sublime.

Atwill's deep, hollow voice pitched to a remote, non-existent gallery is guaranteed to send shivers down the spines of his fellow actors. His delivery of 'Why, isn't this the gentleman from England, Captain Mumm?' is slow, precise, with every comma emphasised and a rising note of wonder on 'Why' to the reverberating boom of 'Captain Mumm'; he makes the line sound even more fake than it is – if that's possible.

A note on the preposterous name, 'Captain Mumm'. I am sure both the writer and director must have been consumed with delighted laughter when they came up with it. It is a name worthy of MacGonagall in its rich, reverberating hollowness. Yet it is a name a bunch of actors would have invented. It rolls nicely off the tongue and into the gutter. Captain Mumm, Mumm, Mumm – once heard, never forgotten.

Colonel 'Concentration Camp' Ehrhardt is a comic version of Bertolt Brecht's poem 'Mask of Evil' which describes a Japanese carving of an evil demon on his wall. Brecht observes 'The swollen veins of the forehead indicating/What a strain it is to be evil.'

Ehrhardt's swollen veins, pop-eyes, twitching walrus moustache and nervous bonhomie shows just what a strain it is for him too. The false heartiness, followed by the hollow chuckle, show a man trying to cope with a part that is too big for him. In life, Colonel Ehrhardt is not a star. The fake Ehrhardt carries it off better because Joseph Tura, whatever they say about him, is one.

To Be or Not to Be is Lubitsch's darkest film and his warmest, second only to *The Shop around the Corner*. That is, in part, due to Ruman. His playing is more subtle than Zero Mostel's in *The Producers* (1967) but cut from the same, broad, vaudevillian cloth.

Ruman was one of the legion of ethnic character actors who adorned Hollywood films in the 1930s, 1940s and 1950s. He played pompous authority figures in the Marx Brothers' *A Night at the Opera* (1935) and *A Day at the Races* (1937). In Howard Hawks' *"—only angels have wings"* (1939), he is the sad Dutch owner of a clapped-out South American airline. It is a waste of a great farcical talent. You feel he is restraining himself all through the film.

His part in Lubitsch's *Ninotchka* (1939) as Ivanoff, one of the endearingly corrupt Soviet commissars, was much more congenial and went with the grain of his talent. But his apotheosis is *To Be or Not to Be*. Though broader, his comic technique matches Benny in their scenes together. His beady eyes are never still. Because of his nervousness he is always making mistakes – telling anti-Hitler jokes, shooting the wrong men, making a play for a woman he comes to believe is Hitler's mistress. Such displays of bone-headed stupidity and petty meanness of the human spirit are the very bedrock of enduring comedy and are naturally funny. Feel-good works of art which show humanity blossoming on all counts in extreme situations run the risk of becoming cosy and portentous.

Ehrhardt would subscribe to the theory that it does not matter to anyone what you do to get to the top, except to those you hurt, and if you hurt them good, they become bums anyway, and don't count. It is a comforting theory but it promotes the nagging fear that, no matter now much you shout, your colleagues are out to get you. Fear and insecurity reign.

On the other hand, he thinks he is being extraordinarily clever when he puts the fake Professor Siletsky (Tura) in with the real one who happens to be dead. He waits outside with a Gestapo captain, complacently smoking a cigar.

The faces of Colonel Ehrhardt

> CAPTAIN: Colonel, he should have cracked by now.
> EHRHARDT: Give him a little time. Let him enjoy his goose pimples.
> BRANDT: Colonel, do you really prefer this procedure to our usual methods?
> EHRHARDT: Well, I would say with intellectuals the mental approach is sometimes more effective and much quicker.
> BRANDT: But if he shouldn't turn out to be an intellectual?
> EHRHARDT: Then we'll try a little physical culture.

The true horror of this buffoon is that he carries death in his hands, just like his real life prototypes.

Ruman plays everything with a fullness and gusto – film acting is not always minimalist – from his heavy-handed sympathy for Maria Tura's loss of Professor Siletsky … 'Now, now little lady' to his frantic would-be seduction of Maria Tura.

> EHRHARDT: Mrs Tura, I'll give you a bracelet. I confiscated a beautiful one today.
> MARIA: I don't want a bracelet.
> EHRHARDT: I – I – I can make life worth living for you. I can give you extra butter rations – I can give you three eggs a week.

Surprisingly this is a warm, almost sympathetic performance. Just as Brecht observes his demon sympathetically, so we are forced to view our Nazi demon sympathetically – ripe and rancid as he is. Always in a hole and always digging himself in deeper, it doesn't make him less evil, only more understandable. Only a comic performance of genius could have pulled off this trick.

The humour of his cries 'So they call me Concentration Camp Ehrhardt' comes from repetition, but also the subtly different reading of the line. There is an increase in anxiety and desperation as he tries to think of something else to say. He snatches at it as a lifeline as he makes blunder after blunder in his conversation with the fake Professor Siletsky. He makes a joke about the Führer and when the fake Professor Siletsky does not laugh, panics.

> EHRHARDT: Oh, Professor, look here. I was only joking … just repeating what I heard. After all, I never … please don't misunderstand me … You see, I am loyal … I would … Heil Hitler.

'So they call me Concentration Camp Ehrhardt'

We have heard the fake Captain Mumm do this routine in the first scene of the play, as a Gestapo officer.

Once again life imitates art, this time exactly. Only the 'real' Colonel Ehrhardt says the lines with wilder, more expansive fear. He knows the consequences of telling jokes about the Führer. The jokers are shot. Some jokes can kill.

Ruman would have made a great Ben Jonson actor. He is an obsessive. His vices are full-bloodedly on display for all to see. It is upfront acting, full in-the-face comic acting which is very rare in movies: rare because it is very dangerous. It can look fake if not done with total inner conviction. The grotesquery has to be real. It is a great loss that we never saw Sig Ruman play the magnificent libertine, Sir Epicure Mammon, in *The Alchemist* or the fanatic Zeal-of-the-Lane Busy in *Bartholomew Fair*. Perhaps he got his chance afterwards in some actors' heaven, where all the great character actors come into their own and play the leads which their talents so richly deserved.

. . . .

The technical credits are fascinating. The producer credit went to Alexander Korda, which was decidedly odd. The Hungarian producer had tried making films in Hollywood before but only became a success with the crude *The Private Life of Henry VIII* (1933), made in England. After becoming a British subject, he returned to America in 1941 in the middle of the war, with the permission of the British government to complete three movies. He also went into partnership with Lubitsch at United Artists to make *To Be or Not to Be*.

What Korda was really doing in America at this time is a mystery, as the British government did not take kindly to prominent nationals leaving the country and spending desperately needed currency abroad in wartime – to say nothing of the patriotic angle. Aldous Huxley, Isherwood and Auden were attacked for being in America in England's hour of need, and even British actors like Charles Laughton were made to feel guilty.

Korda, however, seems to have been encouraged to make these films in America. The theory is that Korda, like the producer Victor Saville, was actually working as an agent for the British government; he was a close friend of Churchill's. The one fact that does seem to support this theory is that when Korda returned to England at the end of 1942, he was promptly knighted for unspecified reasons. If this spy theory is true, you can bet Korda played the spy game to the hilt, living à la carte, in the best hotels, in LA and New York: like all good Hungarians he was, after all, accustomed to room service. In many ways he went spying like Maria Tura went spying, in his finest gowns and in the best restaurants and hotels.

Alexander Korda's influence on the finished film seems, at best, superficial. His brother, Vincent Korda, is a different matter. His contribution to the success of the film was vital.

He was a wonderful designer and his sets for *To Be or Not to Be* are among his best. They range from the bleak, bombed-out streets of wartime Warsaw in winter, to the ornate, former luxury hotel, now used as the Gestapo headquarters. The wide, carpeted corridors and splendid suites conjure up the stylish, high-society backdrop Lubitsch usually used for one of his sophisticated comedies like *Trouble in Paradise*. But the five-star hotel is now Gestapo headquarters and who knows what blood-stained atrocities are being committed in its discreet luxury rooms.

Gestapo headquarters in most World War II movies are usually depicted as bare, bureaucratic offices with a picture of Hitler on the wall. In fact, just like the stage set we saw at the beginning of the film which we were fooled into believing was real, just because it was a cliché. But the opulent setting of a grand hotel is vital for Maria Tura to function. It is the perfect background for her to swan around in, playing a spy in a magnificent evening gown – the one the theatrical director said was totally inappropriate for a play about Nazi oppression. Yet here it seems totally appropriate because the grand hotels were built to set off such gowns, even if the hotel in question is now being used by the Gestapo. The other major set is the Polski Theatre. Though it is run-down it still has the air of a functioning theatre of the old mid-European school, with a grand staircase, prompt box, drapes and heavy curtains.

Vincent Korda knew that sets must never draw attention to themselves. This is a comedy and therefore the actors stand central and should never be overwhelmed by the sets, music or director. In *Citizen Kane* (1941) the sets reflect Welles' flamboyancy, but the cast has to shout to make themselves heard. Nobody in *To Be or Not to Be* has to shout. They are not competing with anything, certainly not the sets, which are always on a human scale.

The cameraman Rudolph Maté was born in Poland on 21 January 1898 and died in Hollywood on 27 October 1964. He was not offended by *To Be or Not to Be* on behalf of his fellow Poles as so many English and American critics were. Apprenticed to the great cameraman, Karl Freund, his work includes, among others, Dreyer's *La Passion de Jeanne d'Arc* (1927), Hitchcock's *Foreign Correspondent* (1941) and Gene Kelly's mould-breaking *Cover Girl* (1944). But for our purposes it is interesting to see he lit one of Laurel and Hardy's best features, *Our Relations* (1936), so he knew what comedy needed. However dark the background, a cameraman has to light the comics' faces. The audience always has to see their faces, otherwise they can't hear their jokes.

Like the film itself, the photography of *To Be or Not to Be* is 'streaky bacon' – a seamless blending of different styles. The activities of the Resistance, in occupied Warsaw, take place in winter, with deep snow on dark streets, and people back-lit and in cold mist and shadow. In contrast, scenes in the theatre between Lombard and Benny are lighter and warmer. Close-ups and group shots are modelled, in depth. There is no top or high lighting. This is all in contrast to Lubitsch's Paramount movies which were given a sparkling surface. There he worked on a flat plane. But that overall lighting would be totally wrong for the darkness creeping round the edges of *To Be or Not to Be*. On the other hand this darkness could not be allowed to obliterate or encroach on the humanity of the brave clowns.

Rudolph Maté turned director and, unlike many cameramen, became a very good one, with a strong storytelling style. 1950 was his great year when he directed four films; what a wonderful work ethic the old studio system encouraged. *Branded, Union Station, No Sad Songs for Me* and the legendary *D.O.A.*, all in one year. On this form, Maté is a more enjoyable director to watch than the complacent William Wyler or the bloated, postwar George Stevens. Lubitsch was confident enough in his own talent not to be afraid of working with the very best. Films are never made by one man, not even Lubitsch. When the team of writer, cameraman, actors and editor are wrong, we are lumbered with *That Uncertain Feeling* (1941). When they are right, we are blessed with *To Be or Not to Be*.

. . . .

Production of *To Be or Not to Be* began on 6 November 1941, and was completed on the 23 December, although Carole Lombard did a day's work on some stills on New Year's Eve.

However, before the production actually began, there were complicated financial arrangements to negotiate. Now, it is important that readers should understand that the accounts of the financing of particular films come from Oz and are prepared by Munchkins. This applies to the profit or losses they are supposed to make. No-one outside the inner circle of producers and their lawyers really know. All one can do is take an educated guess and read the figures, good and bad, with a healthy degree of scepticism.[19]

Lubitsch signed his contract with United Artists for the film on 5 August 1941. It guaranteed that he 'should not be subject to the supervision or control of any office or employee of any producer except Alexander Korda or any Executive Producer who may succeed Alexander Korda.' This indicated what power and prestige Lubitsch had in Hollywood. He had been a close friend of Korda's for years, and he had brought Korda in on the deal so there would be no interference from that quarter. In any case, Korda was busy with his own films, to say nothing of his à la carte spying for his adopted country. Few directors, however 'hot', then or now, could have got a deal with a guarantee of artistic control like this.

Working for less than his usual salary, Lubitsch got $60,000 up front with another $50,000 payable out of the net profits over the next five years, and twenty-five per cent of any profits after being $130,000 in profit for the studio. Net profit is always fairy gold. Gross profit is real. Net profit rarely exists for those on them in a contract. The most successful films in the history of the cinema never come into net profit, which means profit that remains after the film company has paid off continuous ongoing expenses.

I wrote a small British film in which I had a small percentage of net profit. It cost little to make, was a big success on release and was subsequently sold to television. Yet twenty years later, I still received annual accounts which showed the film was in the red because they had just opened in some dusty fleapit in Peru and had spent $100,000 on publicity.

Lubitsch and Melchior Lengyel were paid $10,000 in October 1941 after the deal was signed: if it hadn't been signed presumably they would have got nothing. The money was split $7,000 for Lengyel and $3,000 for Lubitsch which was more than fair. Edwin Justus Mayer got $2,500 a week to write the shooting script. Given that the average time to write a shooting script would be eight to ten weeks, this is a good rate for the job, though richly deserved. It is noteworthy that Mayer is not on a percentage of the profits. He may not have been offered any or, more probably, had decided there was no profit in film profits and took the money upfront. Nowadays few writers' contracts are on a weekly basis, unless it is a 'polishing' job. Mayer was not polishing a pre-existing script. He was writing a script from a given story. On such assignments, the writer is usually hired to write the script in a certain number of weeks for a set sum of money. It is not done on a weekly basis, relieving the writer of the temptation of stretching his assignment.

Lubitsch had writer approval, cast approval and his usual final cut. Clause Twenty-four of his contract reads: 'The director shall have complete and final control over the production of said photoplay ... and shall have complete and final control over the cutting and editing.' United Artists could only interfere with the picture if the censorship boards wanted changes.

Film directors dream of contracts like this. It gives them the control they are always seeking and are never given. These conditions mean it really is a 'Lubitsch Film'. You can only claim the film is totally yours if you have total control. In no film, since roughly the 1960s, has a director been given this degree of autonomy. Yet as the directors' autonomy grows less and less, more and more films – in fact every film – have the above-the-title tag 'A Joe Doakes Film'.

The producers and distributors never mind giving up the glory as long as the real power stays in their hands. If the director has not got 'complete and final control over the cutting and editing' it can never be truly a director's picture.

Jack Benny, a big radio star then, got $125,000 plus ten per cent of the distributors' world gross in excess of $1.25 million. Now this percentage means something. It was a good deal for Benny but he was eager to do the film anyway; he wanted to work with Lubitsch. He considered him 'the greatest comedy director that ever lived'. The only other director he would have given an automatic 'yes' to was Leo McCarey. Benny was always a class act.

Lombard got $75,000 in cash, upfront. The actress was to be paid an additional $75,000 out of a percentage of the producer's profit.

On 26 August, United Artists formed Romaine Film Corporation with a loan from the Bank of America for $1.2 million. Lombard's tragic death necessitated some slight re-editing of *To Be or Not to Be* which added $35,000 to the budget. The cost of the film came in at $1,022,000. Not cheap but not expensive, given the look and quality of the product.

The film was released on 6 March 1942, and on 30 June, United Artists dissolved Romaine Film Corporation while the film was still playing. They adopted the 'cost recovery basis' for calculating the financial returns. This meant that they deducted their costs from the gross so that they could receive their negative costs before reporting any income on the books. In other words, they had covered themselves whatever the film did at the box office.

By taking their cut from the gross income *before* the figures for the takings were complete, United Artists naturally ensured that they would declare a loss on the film because they had already hacked off their negative costs from the total. This so-called 'loss' was despite the fact that the film's worldwide gross was $2.1 million which would, under the Oz-like film accounting system, have produced a profit of over $300,000.

Lubitsch was not paid the remaining $50,000 due to him until 1943, by which time United Artists had been drawing a handsome bank interest for over a year. It's a sweet setup; dealing with film finances is a no-win situation even for a powerful figure like Lubitsch. Lombard's estate only got $57,307 of the net profits to which she was entitled.

The Internal Revenue Service took United Artists to court over tax evasion on this matter. The company said the film had made no profits. They then had to admit they had indeed reluctantly paid Lubitsch his $50,000 and Benny $58,000 as their share of profits, which they had tried to make the tax people believe did not exist.

The government charged that Romaine Film Corporation owed taxes totalling at least $74,067.21. After a great deal of bargaining between lawyers, this was reduced to $21,746.41. The case dragged on until February 1949 when the court declared that United Artists owed the government $11,200 along with a twenty-five per cent penalty.

I am rather inclined to believe that all these figures, for a change, are more or less accurate. The financial manoeuvres have the smell of truth. What finally convinces me is the petty penalty – the $11,200 that United Artists got away with. When you consider that even according to their own books, the film grossed $2.1 million, and even after they had taken out their slice, it made a profit of over $300,000, a piddling $11,200 penalty is par for the course. Never take a film company to court. You lose when you win, they win when you lose.

. . . .

The actual production of *To Be or Not to Be* seems to have gone smoothly. Every film Lubitsch ever made came in on or under budget which was one reason why he never had too much difficulty making another movie. He was trusted not to waste money.

He shot quickly, only running to two or three 'takes' a shot. However he was quite prepared to shoot more to get what he wanted. The silent scene with Benny finding Stack sleeping in his bed went to thirty takes before he was satisfied. The scene still does not work as well as it should but perhaps this is because one knows it had problems. It is covered with 'Mickey Mouse' comic music which indicates Lubitsch was still not happy with it even in post-production and tried to paper the cracks. He needed 'looks' from Benny but for once was unable to get the exact 'looks' he wanted.

When we learn that a scene in a film caused the director difficulties, we watch it more closely. Like the trick knife-throwing shot in Stroheim's *Greed* (1925), it never seems quite right.

All the production stills of the film show the crew laughing. This is rare, especially on a comedy, which can be a grinding business. Marcel Varnel, the best comedy director we ever had – he directed most of the Crazy Gang and Will Hay films, including one comedy masterpiece, *Oh, Mr Porter!* (1937) – had an order that the crew were not to laugh out loud when he was directing. He felt if they were not careful they would start laughing at 'in-jokes' which would not be funny to the audience and he would lose any idea what was working comedically and what was not. Lubitsch obviously did not subscribe to this theory and together with another master craftsman, Leo McCarey, liked to keep the atmosphere on the set bubbling.

The film was released in America on 6 March 1942. The director who was often criticised for concentrating on romantic, boudoir comedies was now dumped on for taking on a serious subject. The critic Bosley Crowther, of the *New York Times*, reviewing *To Be or Not to Be* on 29 March, called the film 'a callous comedy' ... 'a shocking compression of realism and romance' ... shocking obviously to Mr Crowther ... 'Frankly, this corner is unable even remotely to comprehend the humour' ... that was obvious ... 'You might almost think Mr Lubitsch had the attitude of anything for a laugh' ... and so on and so on. The review gives off a feeling of total incomprehension and if a critic cannot comprehend something, it is always the artist's fault, never his own lack of intelligence and sensibility.

Remember, when dealing with critics and criticism, that criticism is just an exchange of opinion and has no authority in relation to the activities it criticises. On the whole, it is a parasitic addendum on art, by men and women who are rarely committed.

When the film was released in England, the reviews suffered from the usual lack of perception, particularly from 'name' critics. They are worth quoting, for they stand as typical of the general reaction from the cultural establishment.

First the two duchesses of film criticism, Misses Lejeune and Powell (1930s to 1960s), who were always bland, predictable and snobbishly middle-brow.

The *Observer* film critic, C. A. Lejeune wrote on 3 May 1942:

The film has brilliantly funny touches, besides some moments of extremely knowing melodrama. It is probably the late Carole Lombard's best piece and I dislike it intensely. To my mind, a farce set against the agonies of bombed Warsaw, is in the poorest of tastes, especially as the film makes no attempt to ignore them [should it have done? surely this would have been in truly bad taste] ... rather indulging, now and then, on a personally conducted tour of the ruins [personally conducted? by whom? probably the fake Hitler] ... Perhaps we in England are too close to the real thing to take a detached view [being close or far away is surely not the point. The only way to do comedy is to take a detached view. The greatest British satirists from Ben Jonson to Jonathan Swift always took such a view] ... At any rate I feel convinced that this is a film we could never have made in this country [absolutely; not then, not now] and much though I covet the Lubitsch technique for our studios, I am very glad we couldn't.

We couldn't and didn't. A more philistine comment it would be difficult to conceive. No wonder British movies have always been, with rare exceptions, technically primitive and their subject matter timid and parochial.

Dilys Powell reviewed the film for the *Sunday Times* on 3 May 1942. After describing the plot of the film in some detail, she went on to ask:

> Well, is the joke funny? Or shall we put it like this: are the actors funny? They are. Jack Benny is funny as an actor in an unrehearsed role; a smart piece of casting on the part of Lubitsch ... Sig Ruman is funny as the Gestapo chief, Lionel Atwill is funny as the standard heavy, Carole Lombard, as the actress playing decoy, gives a performance good enough to make us regret we shall not see her smooth, casual comedy again (this, of course, was the last picture she made before her death). The Lubitsch marital comedy is funny. The Hitler joke is funny. But I repeat: is the joke funny? is the background of terror in Poland funny, with its constant reminders of the frightful reality? Hitler in Ruritania, yes, but the Gestapo in Poland, no. All right, call me Crabapple Annie. But I find myself wondering how America just now would take a brilliant bit of farce about Pearl Harbor; and how we in this country should react to a perfect scream about the fall of Hong Kong?

Miss Powell need never have worried on that score. It would have been impossible for us to make a 'brilliant bit of farce' about Pearl Harbor, or a 'scream' about the fall of Hong Kong. We have never had the courage to make such movies. The English character is too complacent and servile to embark on such projects. Our contribution to World War II movies is that patronising piece of propaganda *In Which We Serve* (1942) – God help us!

It is noteworthy that both critics use exactly the same technique of building up the picture in the beginning of the review, only to knock it down in the last paragraph, not by saying it fails artistically, but by telling us it should never have been made in the first place.

In 1987 Dilys Powell tried belatedly in the *Sunday Times Magazine* to redeem the situation. She wrote:

> It was easy to misjudge this comedy when it was first shown forty years ago ... the disapproval reckoned without the Poles

themselves: those who escaped from Poland liked the movie. Ernst Lubitsch who, with Melchior Lengyel wrote and produced and directed the film had been right all along …

Miss Powell never mentions that she was one of those who vehemently disapproved of the film. She disowned her part in its shameful dismissal.

It is interesting that she only mentions Lubitsch and Lengyel in connection with the screenplay. No critic said a word about the true writer, Edwin Justus Mayer. He might not have existed. So it still goes. The public may not read film credits but it is surely part of a critic's job to know who did what.

These pieces by Lejeune and Powell are crass and totally beside the point but at least both tried to grapple in a bemused way, with something beyond their critical capabilities. But the real cherry on the cake, the most obnoxious, bone-stupid contemporary review of *To Be or Not to Be* appeared in the *New Statesman*, on 2 May 1942, by Roger Manvell. The *Statesman* was a once fiery, impeccable, leftwing weekly; then the intellectuals' bible. It is still with us and still getting it wrong on the arts page. Manvell was a respected elder statesman of film criticism, and wrote several books on the history of the film, all in hard covers. I quote in full his review of *To Be or Not to Be*:

> *To Be or Not to Be* is also a film about resistance in an occupied country – Poland. It is anti-Nazi and skilful, and I suppose funny. But jokes connected with concentration camps in Poland and the execution of Polish patriots seem to me inexcusable, especially when contrived in Hollywood by Messrs Lubitsch and Lengyel, who by birth, I fancy, are respectively German and Hungarian.

As he is into racial smearing, it's a wonder he did not mention they were both Jewish. This is frankly a disgusting review: cheap and ignorant. This critic is a saloon-bar little-Englander. The review has nothing to do with the film discussed and everything to do with the reviewer's ignorant prejudice against Hollywood and all its works. Even his praise 'I suppose funny' becomes a superior European sneer.

I have often wondered why so many so-called heavyweight critics make such a cock-up when dealing with the popular or low arts. There is still a division between high and low art – nobody mentions middle art. I suppose there is some deeply ingrained cultural snobbery at work but there is also something more at the heart of it; a feeling that the material they are commenting on, be it a film, popular music, radio or television is somehow not worthy of their talents. Many despise the material and despise themselves for having to write about it. The obvious solution is to get another job.

If anyone had any doubts about the value of the *Cahiers du Cinéma* boys, you only have to read these sad reviews to know how much they were needed. Later a great deal of silliness was committed in their name but they blew to pieces this sort of empty, complacent film criticism forever, and for that we should be grateful.

After some thirty years in the theatre, one of the best contemporary theatrical notices I ever received was in a weekly, one-page, gay broadsheet called *QX*. It was brilliant, incisive and truly original and was signed 'artbitching by Sasha Selavie'.

So it is with *To Be or Not to Be*. The insightful reviews are to be found in popular magazines and obscure publications.

Today's Cinema for 1 May 1942 had an enthusiastic piece on the film from 'C. A. W.':

> A tongue-in-the-cheek yarn which, being set in Poland, cannot entirely escape a hint of tragedy and pathos. For the most part, however, the narration genially pokes fun at Hitler and Shakespeare impartially, the former in an hilarious series of gags and innuendoes in what is known as the Lubitsch manner. On the comedy action side, we have the atrocities of the hero's Hamlet, amiably summed up by a Nazi character who remarks 'What he did to Shakespeare, we're doing to Poland!' ... it is delightfully portrayed by Jack Benny ... and the late Carole Lombard, provocative and piquant as his superbly helpful wife.

However, another anonymous review, signed D. E. B., in the British Film Institute's *Monthly Film Bulletin* for 1942, really hits the bullseye, clean and true, and is worth quoting in full as a belated tribute to a real critic who got the essence of it right, first time.

> This film is no thoughtless excursion into the doubtful humours of war. Some people, indeed, may think the agony of Poland altogether an improper subject for comedy. For those who do not, good as are the actors, it is the Lubitsch direction which gives it special distinction. He has chosen to take the standpoint of a civilised adult, on the utter idiocy of war. These strutting fools

marching into a beautiful historic city are not to be feared, only to be infinitely despised. He proceeds to despise them with every inch of his film and he achieves his purpose. Many, more serious, films make us half unwillingly admire Nazi efficiency and fanaticism, this apparent comedy barbs its shafts with subtle poison; we see a machine which can be broken and men who can be human and stupid, as well as brutal. Carole Lombard brings the right touch of apparent casualness to her role; Jack Benny is magnificent as Joseph Tura. There is wit, surprise, drama and suspense all through.

Most of the contemporary reviews were particularly incensed by Colonel Ehrhardt's famous comment on Joseph Tura's acting: 'What he did to Shakespeare, we are doing now to Poland.' Only C. A. W. of *Today's Cinema* treated the joke sensibly.

The controversy went right back to the preview of the film. Walter Reisch, Lubitsch's friend remembers the first preview audience which had been bubbling with laughter up to that point, reacted in stunned silence to the audacity of the gag.[20] Afterwards at a nearby restaurant, it turned out that Lubitsch's other friends, Charles Brackett, Billy Wilder,

'What he did to Shakespeare, we are doing now to Poland'

Henry Blanke, S. N. Behrman, and producer Alexander Korda, equally hated the line. Finally Lubitsch's wife asked him to take it out. Everyone present vigorously agreed. Lubitsch was furious. Those present had never seen him so angry. In fact, he rarely, if ever, lost his temper. He defended the line as if an attack on the joke was an attack on the film. It was. He knew it was not just an expendable joke. What he didn't know was that he was, at that moment, surrounded by a group of arch compromisers.

But Lubitsch fortunately didn't listen to the nay-sayers. Edwin Justus Mayer had written it in the script. And if it was in the script, it stayed. I say Mayer had written it; on the evidence that it sounds like Mayer's in its polished savagery. It could have come straight out of his play, *Children of Darkness.*

All the reviewers were incensed by the joke, as they were meant to be. To equate the atrocities an actor committed on a Shakespeare play to the atrocities the Germans committed on the Polish people is still shocking. But it points to a secret correspondence between murdering language and murdering men, women and children. The Austrian satirist, Karl Kraus, predicated what Adolf Hitler would do to Germany by his misuse of a comma in one of his speeches. If he could do that to the German language, he could do it to the German people.

It is odd that nobody seemed to object to another 'shocking' exchange between Tura and Colonel Ehrhardt, when Tura tells the Colonel he is called 'Concentration Camp Ehrhardt' and Ehrhardt replies with a merry chuckle, that the Germans do the 'concentrating' and the Poles do the 'camping'. It is a chilling comic line, the comedy heightened by the fact there is an awful lot of 'camping' going on in the Polski Theatre and beyond.

. . . .

I believe what really shocked contemporary critics was that the 'he did to Shakespeare' line confirmed, beyond a doubt, that Lubitsch was not going to be serious about a serious subject. They could not see he and his writer were being serious by being funny. As in all the best comedy, the seriousness is *in* the comedy, not outside it. Every good joke must be a small revolution. In the great classic comedies of stage, film or novel, the jokes and gags in themselves contain the deeper meaning critics crave. It's why citing Nietzsche and Freud, men not noted for their hilarious humorous routines, cannot explain comedy because they don't see its deeper meaning lies in being funny. Comedians are at their most serious, most meaningful, when they are at their funniest. In the end, I believe, the only thing in the theatre that has the ring of truth is comedy.

Great comedy isn't there to help to make the serious stuff easy to swallow. Comedy *is* the serious stuff. A work isn't great despite the comedy. It's great because of the comedy.

There had been few black comedies up to 1942, particularly in the silent period, except for some of the acrid films of the great Raymond Griffiths like *Hands up* (1926) where at one point he is too busy playing dice with Red Indians to notice that his future father-in-law is being burnt at the stake.

In the sound period there was Sacha Guitry's immoral essay, *Le Roman d'un tricheur* (The Story of a Cheat, 1936), and Marcel Carné's surreal *Drôle de dame* (1936) with an animal rights serial killer going around, slaughtering butchers. As its high point it has Louis Jouvet as a confused English bishop, muttering 'Bizarre, bizarre', and Jean-Louis Barrault parading around in the nude – and a pretty sight he is too! There were black comedies after the war, with *Monsieur Verdoux* (killing for money – 1947), *Kind Hearts and Coronets* (killing for a title – 1949), *The Criminal Life of Archibald De La Cruz* (serial killing – 1955), *El* (madness – 1952) and the neglected *Miss Tatlock's Millions* (incest and madness – 1948).

But as the famous black farce *Arsenic and Old Lace* was enjoying a mammoth hit on Broadway in the 1940s, I do not believe the problem with *To Be or Not to Be* was only the content. What baffled the critics was its style. Or rather styles. If Lubitsch was taking risks with his subject matter, he took even more by mixing styles. Critics hate this more than ineptitude.

Almost one whole reel of the film is devoted to showing the growth of the Resistance to German occupation, when Lieutenant Sobinski escapes to England and joins the RAF before being parachuted back into occupied Poland. This is filmed straight: no jokes. This sequence could have come out of any American war film of the period. There are no visual or verbal jokes unless you include the narrator's over-heated encouragement to 'Kill, kill, kill!'. Actually the narrator continually undercuts the straight visuals by being sonorous and over-ripe. He obviously belongs to the Rawitch school of dramatic acting.

The war footage is one of the bravest of Lubitsch's touches. The deliberate refusal to inject humour is stretched to the limit. By the end of it we have almost forgotten the film is a comedy. The temptation to the

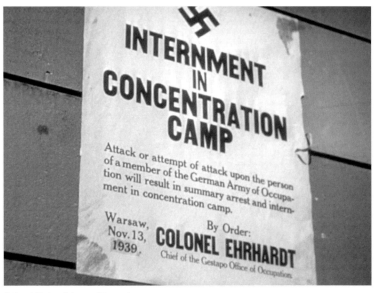

Colonel Ehrhardt leaves his mark

Husband and wife say goodbye to Sobinski, her would-be lover

writer and director to put in something funny must have been well-nigh irresistible. It says much for Lubitsch's pacing and his ability and clout that he could go his own way without caving into the dictates of the front office.

These action sequences are shot in a slightly different style from the rest of the picture. They are dark, misty or oatmeal grey to fit in with the feel of a documentary. There are few close-ups and many long shots and group shots. It is in the style of a Raoul Walsh war picture.

The assassination of Professor Siletsky on the stage of the Polski Theatre on the other hand, after having been hunted through the deserted auditorium, is filmed with the hard-edged, mathematical camera placements of Fritz Lang – a passing thought, does anyone want to consider a comparison between the dry, Lang camera style and Buster Keaton? But it must be added, though this is Lang territory, it is comedy Lang, if the words aren't a contradiction in terms, though, of course, parts of *Moonfleet* (1955) hint that the monocled German did have a sense of humour.

The professor is gunned down, unseen, behind the front curtain; another ellipsis, another 'Lubitsch touch'. When the curtain goes up, Professor Siletsky stands, mortally wounded, in a spotlight in the old

Trapping a German spy à la Fritz Lang

Gestapo set. He sways theatrically, raises his hand in a farewell Nazi salute and manages to gasp 'Heil ... ' before crashing to the ground. The sheer dramatic panache of such a death is duly appreciated by the actors in the auditorium: the shot, the rising curtain and the salute, the gasp and the fall, have been noted and will appear, no doubt, in some future cheesy production at the Polski Theatre.

Melodrama, documentary, slapstick, farce and high comedy come smoothly mixed in *To Be or Not to Be*. The critics objected that it was vulgar, inappropriate and worst of all, new. It wasn't. Such mixing, such jarring styles, goes back to Euripides' *Helen*; and Charles Dickens who loved using the technique. He called it 'streaky bacon'.

Lubitsch himself wrote in the *New York Times* (29 March 1942):

I was tired of the two established, recognised recipes, drama with comedy relief, and comedy with dramatic relief. I made up my mind to make a picture with no attempt to relieve anybody from anything, at any time; dramatic when the situation demands it, satire and comedy whenever it is called for. One might call it a tragical farce or a farcical tragedy – I do not care, and neither do the audience.

But the battle continues. The mixture of styles is still considered suspect by critics (but not by audiences), not only in movies, but in the even more antediluvian theatre.

. . . .

'Satire' is the technical word for writing about people as they are. 'Romantic' at the other extreme is writing about people as they are to themselves. Both of these terms are true and mean something, and Lubitsch combined them in most of his films. Only 'Naturalism' is a completely vague term, and Lubitsch had no truck with it. The trick for a good director or writer is to distance their work from clapped-out narrative forms and the deadly language of journalism.

A director like Lubitsch can have a true, personal style which resides in his surface signature or voice. It is an apparently frivolous surface which turns, in the end, into living truth. His style is based on understatement. Understatement is rarely used nowadays. What is the point when there are so few people who are prepared to listen to anything?

Lubitsch's plots are ingenious, sometimes absurd, but no more absurd than the plots which structure our lives at home or work. What would really be absurd is to think we could bear life without an ingenious plot or two. For life tends to be an artifice. We are born into stories, created by others, and we can only tinker a bit with the details before we die, hopefully leaving a few stories of our own behind.

To Be or Not to Be contains many examples of what came to be called the famous 'Lubitsch touch'. This is merely a method of telling a story through ellipses. Important scenes happen off-screen, on the other side of the film frame, or behind walls or closed doors. Avoiding the obvious, Lubitsch substitutes half-glimpsed details, suggestions, fades, dissolves, blackouts or nothing at all. An American film censor once complained 'You know what he's saying, but you just can't prove he's saying it.'

This is an Emmental cheese approach to film narrative. The holes or empty spaces are deliberately manufactured. Lubitsch empty spaces have a mysterious power. Vermeer's empty spaces have that same power, without the laughs. Lubitsch leaves so much to the imagination, he will always speak to us. The paradox of his work is that it is so elegant and yet so taciturn.

These touches or holes can appear anywhere in the film. In *Monte Carlo* (1930) they are at the opening with Jeannette MacDonald running to catch a train in her underwear. The only explanation she gives to the conductor is that she has just been to a wedding. She then trills 'Beyond the Blue Horizon'. Later we find out she has indeed been to a wedding – her own. But she cannot face marrying the ineffectual groom, Duke Otto von Liebenheim (Claude Allister). It transpires this isn't the first time she has left him at the altar. The duke's response is to tell the assembled guests he is going to get her back 'caveman style', and then he warbles 'She'll Love Me and Like It'.

Often we, the audience, do not get an explanation of the empty spaces. We have to fill them in ourselves which is much more stimulating exercise than just lying back and letting the director and writer try to do all the work.

Lubitsch touches are usually assumed to be exclusively sexual. Many are, but they also touch darker matters like betrayal or death. The climactic unmasking of Marlene Dietrich's 'Belle de Jour'-like Angel happens in a fade-out. The whole film of *Angel* (1937) is predicated on her nostalgia for her early days as a high-class prostitute. Yet words like 'prostitute' are never spoken although much of the film takes place in a discreet brothel. Death and sex is given the touch in *Heaven Can Wait* (1943) where Don Ameche as Henry Van Cleve, the philandering hero, lays on his deathbed, while the camera hovers outside death's door. A beautiful night nurse goes inside. We hear a surprised cry from the nurse as Henry makes a last pass, before gasping his last. We have seen nothing, imagined everything.

There is a particularly daring narrative ellipsis or hole in *To Be or Not to Be*. Lieutenant Sobinski has been parachuted back into occupied Poland. He is to contact the Resistance at a bookshop in Warsaw, and give them Professor Siletsky's photograph, so they can kill him before he betrays them.

We focus on the bookshop and the snow-covered street. Lieutenant Sobinski appears, heads for the bookshop, but then is challenged and chased off by German soldiers. We remain focused on the street. After a dissolve, Maria Tura appears and goes into the bookshop and gives the bookseller Professor Siletsky's picture. She goes back to her apartment, only to be picked up by the Gestapo. Later Joseph Tura comes back to find Lieutenant Sobinski sleeping in his bed.

What has happened 'off-screen' is that after being chased away, Lieutenant Sobinski went to Maria Tura and told her about his mission. She hid him in the apartment and went to the bookshop herself. Perfectly clear, perfectly logical, but we, the audience, do not see any of that plot.

Tura finds Sobinski in his bed

Lubitsch skips, or drills a hole there, confident the audience will fill in the required details. Amazingly, we do. I write 'amazingly' because you would have thought in telling the story we would have had to see Lieutenant Sobinski going to Maria Tura and explaining everything. It's not needed. What *is* needed is Joseph Tura finding Lieutenant Sobinski, his wife's would-be lover, in his bed and his slippers.

There is also another, splendid, Lubitsch death-door 'touch' in *To Be or Not to Be*. Colonel Ehrhardt, in his own inept fashion, is trying to seduce Maria Tura with offers of black market goodies when the actor Bronski, disguised as Hitler, because Joseph Tura's moustache has blown off, bursts in. Colonel Ehrhardt assumes it is the real Hitler and Maria is his mistress. Bronski flees with Maria running after him shouting 'Mein Führer! Mein Führer!' Ehrhardt in his humiliation reaches for his revolver.

The camera discreetly withdraws outside the room and focuses on the closed door. There is a pause. The pauses are important, giving the audience time to picture the scene which they can't see even more vividly than if they could. A shot rings out. Ehrhardt, for the first time in his life, has done the decent thing and shot himself. There is the sound of his body hitting the floor. Another pause, shorter this time, and Ehrhardt's ghostly voice bellows 'Schultz!' He is, as usual, putting the responsibility for another cock-up on his assistant, Captain Schultz (Henry Victor).

Now, film-making has become more literal. Everything is shown, nothing revealed. Yet film is at its most exciting when it does not explain, most boring when it does. Don Siegel, a director of thrillers, not comedies, wrote:

> The more you describe, analyse and *explain* a character, the less real he or she becomes. The trick is to *suggest*, to try to leave holes, problems, questions, that the viewer's imagination will fill in, in a much more satisfying way than we could ever do.[21]

Colonel Ehrhardt's inept suicide is particularly delicious because it could be read in a totally different way. He could have shot himself but given his normal incompetence, made a mess of it and missed. Having wounded himself, he naturally shouts for Schultz, the perpetual scapegoat. Both readings are funny.

The Lubitsch touch involved telling a story visually. Lubitsch was a brilliant silent film director with at least one silent masterpiece, *The Marriage Circle* to his credit. Silent film directors who continued into the sound era had a great advantage; talk was a bonus but they didn't depend on it to further the narrative. This was done with pictures. Actually, there were always many different 'touches'. There was the Ford touch (long shots), Vidor touch (figures in a landscape), Lang touch (objects), Renoir touch (all in one). But, in the end, with all this talk of the Lubitsch touch, it is important to remember the glories he left in were more important than what he left out.

. . . .

Lubitsch's style changed over the years. This was perhaps more to do with studios he worked for, than anything internal, though his last films have an extra richness. At Paramount he used a flat plain, no deep focus, at MGM he was smooth and opulent, for United Artists he used more depth of focus, for 20th Century-Fox there were beautiful box sets and darker shadows. The atmosphere of a typical Lubitsch film isn't like any other. There seems to be a sprinkling of gold-dust in the air. Yet even that changed. With *To Be or Not to Be* the gold-dust turned to sleet and snow. Though, despite everything, the sun still shone, there is now a bracing nip in the air.

Remy de Gourmont declared 'Freely to write what he chooses, is the sole pleasure of a writer.' That is not a freedom given to many American directors or scriptwriters. Lubitsch came as near to that blessed state as any. He was trusted by Hollywood studio executives. He knew how to talk to them and he had class. Studio heads used to like a 'bit of class', provided it came in on budget; the class given to them by great directors was a marketable asset for the company.

For a brief period Lubitsch was even made Head of Production at Paramount. He was the only truly creative artist to run a major Hollywood studio. But it did not work out. Never ask those in power for anything, they might give it to you.

One of the pitfalls of black comedy, comedy on the edge, good taste in bad taste, is a certain coldness. The writer has to be heartless without losing heart. In movies, the audience will tend automatically to identify with the central character. This creates problems if the lead is a serial killer; especially if they are damned and laughable. The film has to be ruthless. *Monsieur Verdoux* is given a heart by the life-affirming vulgarity of Martha Raye, and Dennis Price's love for his mother infuses *Kind Hearts and Coronets*. With *To Be or Not to Be* it is Tura's acting company that provides the identifying humanity. Their solidarity, their pride in their profession warms the movie.

Actually Lubitsch's whole oeuvre can be divided into warm and cold. The cold films include *Bluebeard's Eighth Wife* (cold and unfunny – 1938), *That Uncertain Feeling* (ditto – 1941) and *Angel* (icy). Among the warm ones are *Ninotchka* (1939), *The Shop around the Corner* and *Cluny Brown*.

Paradoxically, in *To Be or Not to Be* the warmth is generated not only by the comradeship of the actors, but also by the gusto of the German villains; Captain Schultz's perennial straight man and fall guy, the two thug-like Gestapo torturers, and Sig Ruman's Colonel Ehrhardt. This dangerous monster is straight out of vaudeville. He is in part W. C. Fields in his eternal suspicions, and Phil Silvers in his undying energy. No-one ever got within miles of it except, perhaps, a French actor, Francis Blanche in *Babette s'en va-t-en guerre* (1959), who is such a fanatical Nazi he even suspects Hitler of not being fascist enough.

Colonel Ehrhardt has a number of moments when he is almost – no, he is – endearing.

Tura, disguised as Professor Siletsky, is confronted with the corpse of the real Professor Siletsky. He suggests to Ehrhardt that maybe the corpse is really a fake.

The fake Professor Siletsky meets the real one – dead

Trying to pull the dead Siletsky's beard

> EHRHARDT: Why don't you convince yourself? Why don't you pull his beard?
> TURA: I can't do it.
> EHRHARDT: So, you can't eh? Too sensitive, eh? You can murder a man … you can kill in cold blood, but you can't pull a man's beard.

Ruman roars out this last speech in a burst of righteous indignation. This from a Gestapo chief who has been shooting men daily for telling jokes. Like the rest of us, his anger blinds him to the rich absurdity of a line like 'you can kill in cold blood, but you can't pull a man's beard'.

Near the end of the film, Ehrhardt and Schultz visit Maria Tura with something urgent to discuss.

> SCHULTZ: The Colonel and I … we were talking things over. Mrs Tura we consider you a woman of enormous appeal.
> MARIA: Thank you. But what's so urgent about that?
> SCHULTZ: It struck me as rather peculiar why anybody like you could be, shall we say … attracted to Professor Siletsky.
> MARIA: Oh, Captain, you never can tell about these things …

Ehrhardt, who is standing behind Maria, looks sage at this moment as if he knows all about women's taste.

> MARIA: For instance, I think you're rather attractive yourself, Captain …

Ehrhardt's face registers total surprise now. Indeed how could the super attractive Maria Tura find anything attractive in his lumpen assistant?

> MARIA: Perhaps my taste is a little peculiar.

Ehrhardt nods vigorously in agreement.

In his mind Maria certainly has peculiar tastes if she is attracted to Schultz. Ehrhardt's changes of expression are boldly registered. It is immoral but we identify with him at this moment and laugh. For his obvious implication is; how could a woman like Maria Tura find Captain Schultz attractive, next to that fine figure of a man, Colonel Ehrhardt?

But it is Tura's troupe who provide the ballast, the human qualities, with their solidarity and total commitment. The actors are bound together despite personal differences. They may bitch about each other

The company listens to Hitler

but they present a united front against their enemies. When one of their company gets into trouble, the others come to the rescue despite the dangers. Tura and Maria are rescued by the whole company working together. And the whole company escape to England – no-one is left behind. This is what 'fraternity' means.

Like the acting company itself, the marriage of Joseph Tura and Maria is stronger than it appears. Of course, he is a monster of vanity, but he loves his wife, Poland and his bedroom slippers, not necessarily in that order. Together with his fellow actors, he is effortlessly courageous and functions best in situations of high melodrama, like another 'great, great actor', Mark Cardigan (Vincent Price) in *His Kind of Woman* (1951). Naturally, the more dramatic the scene, the more at home they all are. Provided he is the star, and is given his lines, Tura steps smoothly, even lightly, into Gestapo headquarters. No stage fright. It is just another show, another performance.

Maria Tura is a cool lady; flirtatious, vain and beautiful, with all the confidence that ineffable beauty brings. When the company escape to Scotland and her husband is asked what he wants to do, she answers for him with a tender weariness which is very touching, 'He wants to play Hamlet'.

Joseph and Maria Tura quarrel

He is suspicious …

… and has his suspicions confirmed by Siletsky

A rock solid marriage: 'He wants to play Hamlet'

The Turas may knife each other in private, but attacked in public, they stay united. Maria comes on stage at a rehearsal to confront the director Dobosh in a shimmering evening gown.

MARIA: How do you like my dress?
DOBOSH: Very good ... very good. [suddenly realising] Is that what you are going to wear in the ... concentration camp?
MARIA: Well, don't you think it's pretty?
DOBOSH: That's just it.
MARIA: Well, why not? I think it's a tremendous contrast. Think of me being flogged in the darkness ... I scream ... suddenly the lights go on and the audience discovers me on the floor in this gorgeous dress.
GREENBERG: That's a terrific laugh.
DOBOSH: That's right, Greenberg. You keep out of this. That a great star, an artist could be so unartistic! You must be out of your mind.
TURA: What do you mean by talking to my wife like that? How dare you.
DOBOSH: Oh, I'm sorry. I lost my head.
TURA: Sweet, that dress stinks.

Tura has immediately leapt to his wife's defence in public. But in private, in a scathing aside, he puts the knife in and tells her the dress stinks. She naturally puts the rebuke down to professional jealousy. He doesn't like the fact that if she wore the dress, she'd run away with the scene. The fact it is grotesque doesn't occur to her. Or if it does, it's not as important as making her the magnet of a great scene. And it would be a great scene – a great comic scene, as Greenberg pointed out – in appalling taste.

The Tura marriage is rock solid, despite the private sniping. Just as the community spirit of the troupe is unbreakable, despite the private backbiting. Even Rawitch readily puts himself in danger by rescuing Tura, even if he doesn't need it, by passing himself off as Goering's brother-in-law. The unsuspected irony of this bit of business is that after the war, Goering's actual brother turned out to be a courageous anti-Nazi who rescued many Jews from the Gestapo.

. . . .

All the theatrical material in this film is pinpoint accurate, right from the opening scene which seems to take place in Gestapo headquarters. Guards shout a warning.

> OFFICER: The Führer.

Bronski enters, dressed as Hitler.

> EVERYONE: Heil Hitler!
> TURA: Heil Hitler!
> BRONSKI: Heil myself!
> DOBOSH: That's not in the script.
> BRONSKI: But Mr Dobosh. Please!
> DOBOSH: That's not in the script, Mr Bronski!
> BRONSKI: But it will get a laugh.
> DOBOSH: But I don't want a laugh here ...

These are exactly the words I heard a director say to an actor at a rehearsal of a farce. I knew, at that moment, the production was doomed. As Greenberg says later, 'a laugh is nothing to be sneezed at'.

'Heil myself!'

Edwin Justus Mayer's knowledge of the theatre was extensive and it was important that the theatrical background should be true and real, when the plot spirals out into surreal complications. The theatrical background in this movie is the most accurate in any American film. They often get it wrong, especially in the details. Even Joseph L. Mankiewicz's *All about Eve* (1950) is an outsider's view. No theatrical management would ever give an understudy a lead in a new play after having seen only one stage performance. If their preferred star turned down the part, they would have gone to another star actress before entrusting the part to an unknown. It is a detail but significant. Mankiewicz didn't work in the theatre; Edwin Justus Mayer did and Lubitsch had, and always loved it.

> DOBOSH: Mr Bronski, I hired you as an actor and not as a writer, understand? Now what does the script say?
> BRONSKI: I make an entrance.
> DOBOSH: And what do you say?
> BRONSKI: Nothing.
> DOBOSH: Then say nothing!

This sounds absolutely right, if perhaps a touch idealistic. There are not many directors who would be prepared to defend a script with such commendable integrity.

Later, the actors disguise themselves as real Gestapo officials, and the theatrical details remain painfully real. When Tura, impersonating Colonel Ehrhardt, interviews Professor Siletsky, he has to improvise his dialogue. It mainly consists of desperately banal phrases and a repetition of the joke, 'So they call me Concentration Camp Ehrhardt?' Tura isn't a writer, he keeps leaving Siletsky to consult his fellow conspirators in another room. But they have no idea what to do, except for him to keep improvising, until they come up with a solution. But Tura runs out of dialogue. He tells his co-conspirators he's 'dying back there'. Siletsky becomes suspicious and pulls a gun. Tura has betrayed himself, not by making any mistakes, but by running out of believable dialogue.

This insight into the dangers of improvisation for actors is all too real. They aren't writers. After five minutes of improvising their own dialogue, they 'dry'. Nothing comes to mind except endlessly repeated banalities. Watching improvisations, you soon want to pull a gun like Siletsky, and escape.

The fake Ehrhardt meets the real Siletsky

The fake Siletsky meets the real Ehrhardt

The realistic theatre background means that, except for Atwill's Rawitch, the actors are not particularly over-the-top. Certainly not when compared with the Nazis. If Colonel Ehrhardt were to become a member of the troupe, he would be asked to tone down his bug-eyed mannerisms. In a different way, Stanley Ridges' Professor Siletsky is too much the suave George Sanders-like spy, with his neat goatee beard, English tweed suit, charm and impeccable manners. He is the standard theatrical, stereotypical villain, just as Robert Stack's fighter pilot is too much the clean-cut juvenile lead.

Jack Benny can impersonate Colonel Ehrhardt easily because Ehrhardt is another unsleeping paranoiac. In fact, Benny's Ehrhardt is the more convincing Gestapo chief, until he runs out of believable dialogue. He is quietly spoken, authoritative, able to command the space around him like any star. Both Tura and Ehrhardt believe their co-workers are out to get them. Both have to remain vigilant to continue to keep top billing.

The theatrical realism extends to Benny's Hamlet. It is, of course, wonderfully comic; the prissy walk, the limp-wristed campness, the poisonous looks and marbled hair. But it is also a valid interpretation of the part. We see three sequences in which Benny performs his Hamlet on stage, and they are only minimal glimpses of the 'To be or not to be' monologue. But they are enough.

He enters up stage in tights and frilly shirt, reading a book. In the first sequence we see the prompter silently mouthing the most famous line in Shakespeare for him, 'To be or not to be'.

Before he opens his mouth we know who this Hamlet is – an aged, preening, peevish fantasist. The actor has taken a line on how to play the part. He is Jack Benny but also a valid Prince of Denmark who would never be able to revenge the death of his father. So he will procrastinate, make excuses, decking out his weakness with pretentious explanations of the universe. He is too self-absorbed to function properly.

The Hamlets of, say, Kenneth Branagh or Mel Gibson are Branagh and Gibson, mouthing Shakespeare's words. They are themselves. If Shakespeare's character fits their character that's fine; if it doesn't they don't bother. We never really know why Hamlet doesn't get on with the job of killing Claudius. With Benny we do know. He is too busy thinking of himself. This pretentious prig would never look away from the mirror long enough to do anything positive.

The film's emphasis on a realistic theatrical background is important because one of the major themes of the movie is that life, politics, love and death are all show-business. This idea has grown more

Prompter: 'To be or not to be'

Tura as Hamlet

relevant with the passing years. It is modern but also rooted in twentieth-century fascism. The stylised uniforms, the huge rallies, the ranting, spot-lit speeches, the two a.m. knock on the door, were all show-business.

The Nazis were obsessed by the movies, just like the Bolsheviks. Joseph Goebbels, the German Minister of Propaganda, in particular, dreamed of running a Hollywood Studio – MGM would have been ideal for him – and it must be conceded he would have made a good job of it. He certainly would have felt at home in the lethal Byzantine intrigues of a major studio.

In 1943, Goebbels, who started his career as a playwright, gave the order to make a film epic called *Kolberg*. It was to be Germany's answer to *Gone with the Wind* which had literally made him ill with envy.

Kolberg was a massive historical epic which took years to make, and was only 'wrapped' in 1945, in the last months of the war. It consumed unlimited resources. Two hundred thousand troops were drafted from the Eastern Front to appear as extras – and were they glad they were picked. They were in the movies instead of dead in some ditch outside Leningrad. In keeping with Hollywood tradition, the epic scenes in which they appeared were cut out of the final print. The Third Reich collapsed before the film could be released, so prints were parachuted into besieged German cities which were being bombed into extinction.

Those two hundred thousand grateful extras, acting in a fake battle, on a fake battlefield, while the murderous last battle for Germany raged all around, must have wondered what was real and what was show-business, and if there was any difference. On the other hand, perhaps the German extras were only too familiar with the whole situation. Germany under the Nazis was one vast film set, a burning backdrop for their leader's mad dreams. This blurring of the line between theatre and life, living and acting, is what *To Be or Not to Be* is about. It is also about the difference between film and theatre acting.

On the whole, in films, the props – this chair, this table, this fork, this earth, this sky – are real. The only fake things are the actors. In the theatre, props are generally fake, particularly earth and sky. The only real things are the actors. So movie actors have to get their reality from their props. The guns they are holding are real. They just have to be as believable as their props. On stage, the actors have to convince the audience earth and sky, and the knife and fork they handle, are as real as they are.

In *To Be or Not to Be* most of the scenes aren't real; neither are the props or settings. The actors have to convince their enemies they are. That calls for a theatrical style from the actors who pump reality into the scenes they are playing to fool the Gestapo. It is complicated, however, because the non-actors, like Colonel Ehrhardt, are already over-acting, perhaps to compensate for the fact that they do not believe their authority is real.

In Poland in 1942, the Germans have created a surreal universe. The film depicts that brutal dream world in all its horror, and at the same time shows us, comedically, how it can be defeated by making our own dreams stronger, more vivid and alive.

. . . .

It is hard to create time-resistant comedy. Everything changes. Who now laughs at Lancelot Gobbo or Abbott and Costello? Time and hard winters take the shine off the Marx Brothers, so their work seems constipated. It is the idea of the Marx Brothers – or rather, Groucho – that is funny, just as it is the idea of W. C. Fields that has us laughing. I adore his image, laugh at the thought of him, and try to live by his healthy example of undeviating suspicion of humanity. But his films, I hate to say, do not seem to be laugh-makers any longer, except the evergreen *The Face on the Bar Room Floor* (1933).

The sentimental putty holding Chaplin's edifices upright has long since been washed away. Time even affects Keaton. I watch a Keaton film and marvel. I still find scenes funny but mostly, I am too busy gasping in awe at the sheer ingenuity, beauty and breathtaking daring of it all; I forget to laugh.

Of course I'm getting older. But perhaps it is not me or the beloved classic film comedies that have changed but the nature of our laughter. Before, the laughter evoked by a film comedy was always communal. It was created with the community in mind. We laughed in a cinema, with, perhaps because, hundreds of other people around us laughed as well. We laughed together. We laughed with strangers. Now, especially with old movies, the laughter is often solitary. It's like laughing at our own jokes. And people usually do that because they cannot understand any others. We see the great comedies on television, videos or DVDs. We are not swept up onto the comic heights by the gales of laughter of others, who also see the joke. Our solo laughter seems thin in comparison with yesterday's communal 'boffo'.

Now, getting to see the more famous classic films is easy, thanks to videos and DVDs. They are on tap so there is little sense of anticipation. Our familiarity has stilled some of the laughter. Years ago it was more difficult. In England you had to belong to a film society or the National Film Theatre, or you could see some of these films in local independent cinemas. During the late 1950s and 1960s, there were scores of them in London. They ran split weeks: one main feature and a second feature from Monday to Wednesday, then a different programme Thursday to Saturday. A much older film, plus an old second feature was shown on Sunday. You had to criss-cross the capital, to track down movies. That's how I'd find myself in the Ionic, Golders Green, watching *Bringing up Baby* (1938) or in a scruffy cinema in Victoria, watching *Bachelor Mother* (1939), while they 'shot-up' in the toilets. Part of the pleasure was not only in the film, but also in the chase. That's all gone. Everything changes, even our laughter, it seems.

What for me remains laugh-inducing? Well, there is always, without fail, Laurel and Hardy – *the* most enduring film clowns of the twentieth century. They are as eternal as you can get, given our finite lives. After that it's odd-bins: *Hellzapoppin'* (1941), still as fresh as fresh paint, Red Skelton, Fred Allen, Will Hay, Phil Silvers and others. It is all indiscriminately personal, white wine with fish. Lubitsch, of course, and predominantly *To Be or Not to Be*.

In 2001, the National Film Theatre held a season of Lubitsch films. I went to see *To Be or Not to Be* on Saturday 8 December at 8.45 p.m.

Of course I had seen the film often, over the years, on video, and television, but this was the first time I had seen it with an audience for something like ten years. I took two actor friends, Ms Dilys Laye and Mr Peter Bayliss, who had never seen the film before and I was interested in their professional theatrical opinion. I was more than uneasy when I realised the auditorium was only one-third full. The last time I went to the movie, at the same cinema, it was packed.

But the moment the credits rolled and the stirring over-the-top music boomed out, and the first scene in the fake Gestapo headquarters unreeled, all unease vanished. My anxiety, and I was anxious – I wanted everyone to love the film, particularly my friends, as much as I did – vanished. I sat back not to analyse, not to evaluate, not to judge, but to enjoy.

My enjoyment was reinforced by the audience's own. The laughs were still there. The laughter of this audience was not belly-laughs but a continuous bubbling of laughter. This was the laughter of delight, made up of surprise at the ingenuity and audacity of the piece. They laughed at every unexpected twist of the plot. They laughed at the black humour, and the Shakespeare–Poland joke still got the biggest. But this laugh was accompanied by a collective intake of breath. After nearly sixty years, it still had the ability to shock. Lubitsch and Mayer would have been pleased.

As they would have been by my two friends. Thankfully they could not stop laughing, having naturally got every last theatre in-joke. It was Ms Laye who pointed out the joke of Rawitch's crown hitting the overhead lampshade with a clang. She thought this was the essence of nuts-and-bolts theatre, theatre from the inside; while Mr Bayliss noted how contemporary the scene was where the troupe are escaping to England, and the fake Hitler orders the Nazi pilot and crew to jump out of the plane without parachutes. They do, enthusiastically. I had thought this scene a little unreal, but after the attack on the World Trade Centre, it is obvious that followers in the grip of a cause or a charismatic leader will obey any order, however suicidal. Once again, after sixty years, life catches up with art. As it did even when this book was going to press. On 5 May 2002, Jean-Marie Le Pen, the fascist French presidential candidate, held a rally to explain his crushing defeat at the polls as a media plot. As if to confirm his paranoia, one of the many television screens around him began to show *To Be or Not to Be* before a panic-stricken technician could unplug it. For two sublime minutes there was Le Pen wind-bagging on one screen, Tom Dugan's absurd Hitler – the man most Frenchmen compared him to – on another, 'heil-ing' himself. The film's bite remains fresh and ferocious. *To Be or Not to Be* is still news that stays news.

The crew ordered to jump

After the show both friends could not begin to imagine how the film ever got made; its originality and courage had genuinely overwhelmed them. It is true. With all its other transcendent virtues it is the wondrous courage of the film that will continue to shine. That courage is contagious. This is how an artist can and should work, even in movies; no compromise.

What other reasons make it survive, fresh as vintage champagne, after all these years? Maybe it has something to do with the dark undertow of vintage Jewish humour swirling around the basic joke. Jewish jokes are made to endure: 'A rival Jewish comic once told Milton Berle if he had his life to live again he should do it overseas …' Or this. 'How do you like my future bride?' 'She's not what I expected her to be.' 'What did you expect her to be?' 'Blind …'

Or, in keeping with *To Be or Not to Be*'s subject matter, this. After World War II, the aged, fugitive Hitler and Goebbels have survived and are discovered in a New York restaurant when another diner recognises them and goes over. 'Hitler? Goebbels? What're you two doing here?' 'We're creating the Fourth Reich,' says Goebbels. 'It's true,' says Hitler, 'only this time we're going to kill ten million Jews and six postmen.' 'Why're you going to kill six postmen?' asks the diner. Hitler turns to Goebbels in triumph. 'You see, nobody cares about the Jews!'

Along with the Jewish jokes it is the film's vaudevillian toughness that connects it with life as it is lived. The best vaudeville and music-hall comedy was impressed by nothing and nobody: not the law, politicians, sex, old age or death. Most certainly not Hitler ('Heil Hitler … Heil myself') or any uniformed fool or strutting world leader.

Evil is too deep, too natural to the soul to be defeated by comedy but it is brought down to earth, made ordinary and, above all, understandable. We have to survive and use whatever means in our power to stay in the fight. If we're lucky we can turn our flaws as human beings – our conceit, selfishness, vanity – into weapons to defeat those who would make this world a sludge pit. *To Be or Not to Be* shows us how to dissemble, dodge and do back-flips. The exploiters can be fooled, no matter how powerful they seem. Tura and the other heroes are more than a match for the master race. Which is why, in the end, the comedy is so stirring, so exhilarating.

Lubitsch was an exile in a strange land. He had no true home, so his work became a place for him to live. Above all he thought funny. It's a trick of the mind but you have to be born with it. It cannot be learned. Unless you think funny, you can't act, write or direct funny. As a man, Lubitsch loved practical jokes. As an artist he succeeded in not growing up without remaining infantile. Even the most cynical comedian has to retain a certain innocence, otherwise he or she wouldn't find the world worth saving.

After America entered World War II, Lubitsch, a naturalised citizen, became an air-raid warden in Los Angeles. One night Laurence Olivier observed him yelling at a blackout offender, in the thickest German accent he could muster. When they heard his almost impenetrable, guttural bark, the inhabitants of that LA street, long ago, must have truly thought the Germans had already landed and Colonel Ehrhardt had taken control.

To Be or Not to Be reminds us that the theatre precedes reality; it doesn't copy it. The fake is easier to accept than the real thing, which only looks fake, a truth you immediately realise when it hits you in the face. Reality is more theatrical than the theatre. It is why naturalism looks so unreal and comedy so much truer than tragedy, which sentimentalises violence, misery and death and poeticises rotting corpses by calling them noble. The artistic rendering of the physical pain of those who are beaten down with rifle butts and iron bars contains the possibility that pleasure and profit can be squeezed from it. Tragedy makes the unthinkable appear to have some meaning. It becomes transfigured, without the horror being removed, and so justice is denied to the victims. Comedy does not tell such pernicious lies.

Coleridge declared that 'one promise of genius in a poet is the choice of subject very remote from the private interests and circumstances of the writer himself.' In his films Lubitsch creates an off-handed but shimmering comic dream world: not our world, not even his world, but a poet's world. It consists of the best hotels, wines, clothes and five-star room service. I'm sure at this very moment he is dining at the 'Ernst', the best restaurant in Paradise, run, no doubt, by those three Russian rogues, Iranoff, Buljanoff and Kopalski.

In *To Be or Not to Be* this five-star dream turns into a comic nightmare, but its heroes and heroines still retain their sense of style and good manners. Manners for Lubitsch were a sign of human goodness and decency. Without manners and wit you slap your enemy's face to show your superiority and from then on it's downhill all the way, ending in torture and death. Lubitsch believed we live amid surfaces and the true art of life is to skate well on them. For him, even his lightest comedy was never a light matter. It was always too important.

No wonder the first thing the girl (Veronica Lake) says to the film director (Joel McCrea) in Sturges' *Sullivan's Travels* (1942) is 'Did you ever meet Lubitsch?'

NOTES

1 John Barrymore thought a footnote was like the doorbell ringing on your wedding night and you have to go downstairs to answer it. *To Be or Not to Be* was hopelessly remade by Mel Brooks in 1983.

2 *New Yorker*, April 1942.

3 Herman G. Weinberg, *The Lubitsch Touch: A Critical Study* (New York: Dover Publications, 1977).

4 Quoted in James Harvey, *Comedy in Hollywood* (New York: Alfred A. Knopf, 1983).

5 Edwin Justus Mayer, *Children of Darkness: A Tragi-comedy in Three Acts* (London: S. French, 1938), p. 64 (Act 3 Scene 1).

6 2nd edn, ed. by Gerald Martin Bordman (Oxford: Oxford University Press, 1992).

7 See Scott Eyman, *Ernst Lubitsch: Trouble in Paradise* (Baltimore, MD: Johns Hopkins University Press, 1993).

8 Samuel Raphaelson, *Three Screen Comedies* (Madison: University of Wisconsin Press, 1983).

9 See Bernard Taper, *Balanchine: A Biography* (New York: Harper and Row, 1963).

10 For information on A. L. Boasberg, see Ben Schwartz, 'The Man Who Invented Jack Benny', *Written By* [the magazine of the Writers' Guild of America], vol. 6 no. 4, April 2002.

11 See Arthur Frank Wertheim, *Radio Comedy* (New York: Oxford University Press, 1979), which is packed with information about the golden age of radio comedy, complete with extracts from scripts and interviews with the survivors.

12 Fred Allen, *Treadmill to Oblivion* (Boston: Little Brown, 1954) contains a number of Allen's best television comedy scripts plus a wry commentary from the man himself. Even better is his wonderful autobiography, *Much Ado about Me* (Boston: Little Brown, 1956), which contains the richest account – from the inside – of American vaudeville in its heyday.

13 Jack Benny and Joan Benny, *Sunday Nights at Seven* (New York: Warner Books, 1990).

14 Ibid.

15 See Leonard Maltin, *Carole Lombard* (New York: Pyramid, 1976).

16 See Eyman, *Ernst Lubitsch*.

17 See Harvey, *Romantic Comedy*.

18 Ibid.

19 I am grateful to Scott Eyman for providing the financial statements on which my account in this section is based; see Eyman, *Ernst Lubitsch*.

20 See Eyman, *Ernst Lubitsch*.

21 See Don Siegel, *A Siegel Film* (London: Faber and Faber, 1993).

CREDITS

. . . .

To Be or Not to Be

USA
1942

Directed by
Ernst Lubitsch
Produced by
Ernst Lubitsch
Screenplay by
Edwin Justus Mayer [and
Ernst Lubitsch]
Original Story by
Melchior Lengyel
Photographed by
Rudolph Maté
Film Editor
Dorothy Spencer
Production Designed by
Vincent Korda
Musical Score by
Werner R. Heymann

© Romaine Film
Corporation
Production Company
Alexander Korda presents an
Ernst Lubitsch production
Released through United
Artists
Production Manager
Walter Mayo
Technical Supervision
Richard Ordynski
Assistant Directors
William Tummel, William
McGarry
Casting Director
Victor Sutker
Special Effects by
Lawrence Butler
Associate Art Director
J. MacMillan Johnson
Interior Decoration
Julia Heron
Props
Jack Caffey

**Miss Lombard's
Costumes**
Irene
Make-up Artist
Gordon Bau
Sound
Frank Maher
Sound System
Western Electric
Mirrophonic Recording

Cast
Carole Lombard
Maria Tura
Jack Benny
Joseph Tura
Robert Stack
Lieutenant Stanislav
Sobinski
Felix Bressart
Greenberg
Lionel Atwill
Rawitch
Stanley Ridges
Professor Alexander Siletsky
Sig Ruman
Colonel Ehrhardt
Tom Dugan
Bronski
Charles Halton
Producer Dobosh
George Lynn
actor-adjutant [Captain
Mumm]
Henry Victor
Captain Schultz
Maude Eburne
Anna, the maid
Halliwell Hobbes
General Armstrong
Miles Mander
Major Cunningham

[uncredited]
Peter Caldwell
actor-Wilhelm Kunze, Hitler
Youth boy

Armand Curly Wright
make-up man
Ernst Verebes
stage manager
Sven Hugo Borg
actor-German soldier
Olaf Hytten
Polonius in Warsaw
Edgar Licho
prompter
Frank Reicher
Dr Bojalski, Polish official
John Kellogg
Paul Barrett
Gene Rizzi
Maurice Murphy
Polish RAF flyers
Leslie Dennison
captain
Wolfgang Zilzer
M. Sztaluga, bookshop
proprietor
Robert O. Davis
Gestapo sergeant
Roland Varno
pilot
Helmut Dantine
Otto Reichow
co-pilots
Alec Craig
James Finlayson
Scottish farmers
Charles Irwin
Leyland Hodgson
reporters

8,886 feet
99 minutes

Black and White
MPAA: 7834

Credits compiled by
Markku Salmi,
BFI Filmographic Unit

ALSO PUBLISHED

If you would like further information about future BFI Film Classics or about other books on film, media and popular culture from BFI Publishing, please write to:

BFI Film Classics
BFI Publishing
21 Stephen Street
London W1P 2LN

BFI FILM CLASSICS

BFI Film Classics '... could scarcely be improved upon ... informative, intelligent, jargon-free companions.'
The Observer

Each book in the BFI Publishing Film Classics series honours a great film from the history of world cinema. With new titles published each year, the series is rapidly building into a collection representing some of the best writing on film. If you would like to receive further information about future Film Classics or about other books on film, media and popular culture from BFI Publishing, please fill in your name and address and return this card to the BFI.* (No stamp required if posted in the UK, Channel Islands, or Isle of Man.)

NAME

ADDRESS

POSTCODE

E-MAIL ADDRESS:

WHICH *BFI FILM CLASSIC* DID YOU BUY?

* In North America and Asia (except India),
please return your card to:
University of California Press, Web Department,
2120 Berkeley Way, Berkeley, CA 94720, USA

BFI Publishing
21 Stephen Street
FREEPOST 7
LONDON
W1E 4AN